EDITING TEXTS IN THE HISTORY
OF SCIENCE AND MEDICINE

Conference on Editorial Problems

Previous Conference Publications

The title of the 1982 conference is "Editing Polymaths: Erasmus to Russell"; the volume will be edited by H.J. Jackson.

Copies of all previous volumes are available through
Garland Publishing Inc.

EDITING TEXTS IN THE HISTORY OF SCIENCE AND MEDICINE

Papers given at the seventeenth annual
Conference on Editorial Problems
University of Toronto,
6–7 November 1981

EDITED BY TREVOR H. LEVERE

Garland Publishing, Inc.. New York & London

1982

Library of Congress Cataloging in Publication Data

Conference on Editorial Problems (17th : 1981 :
    University of Toronto)
    Editing texts in the history of science and medicine.

    Includes index.
    1. Technical editing—Congresses.   2. Science—His-
tory—Sources—Congresses.   I. Levere, Trevor Harvey.
II. Title.
T11.4.C66   1981   808'.02   82-15800
ISBN 0-8240-2432-X

Printed on acid-free, 250-year-life paper
Manufactured in the United States of America

Contents

Notes on Contributors

BERT S. HALL teaches the history of Technology at the University of Toronto, and has edited *The Technological Illustrations of the so-called "Anonymous of the Hussite Wars"* (Wiesbaden, 1979).

STILLMAN DRAKE is Professor Emeritus of the History of Science at the University of Toronto, and the leading authority on Galileo.

I. BERNARD COHEN is Victor S. Thomas Professor of the History of Science at Harvard University, has edited Newton's *Principia*, and has published widely on all aspects of the scientific revolution.

ARMAND BEAULIEU is editing the Correspondence of Marin Mersenne for the Académie des Sciences and the Centre National de Recherche Scientifique.

LINDA EHRSAM VOIGTS is Associate Professor of English at the University of Missouri-Kansas City, and has published extensively in the history of Medieval Medicine in England.

Introduction
Trevor H. Levere

The Seventeenth Conference on Editorial Problems was devoted to exploring issues in the history of science and medicine. The five papers range from the examination of unpublished technical notes to the clarification of published texts, and from Middle English medical writing and Renaissance technological illustration to Newton's books and manuscripts.

Stillman Drake, in his paper on Galileo's notes on motion, shows how the process of editing leads to insights into the mode and sequence of scientific discovery. The significance of even obscure numerical data and the need for complete editions of manuscripts are recurrent themes in Drake's argument, through which the texture of our understanding of Galileo's work emerges as heavily dependent on the careful chronological arrangement of scattered fragments.

The needs and issues involved in editing Middle English medical texts are addressed in Linda Ehrsam Voigts' paper, which considers problems common to other disciplines of the period, and those especially characteristic of medicine. The difficulties of translation were especially acute for writers faced with new technical terms; the editor's task in establishing texts is particularly challenging when faced with translations of which no Latin exemplar survives. Voigts shows how editing these texts sheds light on the process of translation, the development of written English, and the growth of English medicine.

For the editor and historian of early technology, the lack of a necessary connection between science and technology, and the fact that artifacts rather than texts are the products of technology, offer immediate hurdles. The result is that early technological literature was generally the product of exceptional circumstances, such as the search for court patronage. Bert S. Hall tackles the problems involved in establishing a typology for such literature, and in editing illustrated works where the drawings may be more important than the words.

Words are very much the concern of Armand Beaulieu, who continues to edit the vast correspondence of Marin Mersenne. That correspondence provided the major network of scientific communication in Europe in the years before scientific journals. Beaulieu discusses the location of manuscripts, the establishment and annotation of texts, and the function of the correspondence in the context of seventeenth-century scientific research. The range of subject matter and of personal acquaintance alike are as challenging to the editor as they are welcome to the historian.

In the final paper, I. Bernard Cohen examines the history of the editing of Isaac Newton's writings, beginning with the material that Newton approved for publication; entering a second phase in the nineteenth century with Brewster's biography and its appendices with new texts from manuscript sources; and initiating almost an industry following the auction at Sotheby's and consequent dispersal of some three million words in Newton's hand. The effect of these successive revelations on the study of Newton is Cohen's theme, and the dependence of historiography upon editing is a richly documented conclusion.

The Committee of the Conference on Editorial Problems is grateful to the Social Sciences and Humanities Research Council of Canada for support, and to the University of Toronto for sponsoring the Conference. Thanks are also due to University College, to the Office of the Dean of the Faculty of Arts and Science, and to the Department of English for financial assistance. As convener of this year's conference, I have been gratefully dependent upon the other members of the committee, and especially upon G.E. Bentley, Jr., Hugo de Quehen, Bert S. Hall, H.J. Jackson, Richard Landon, and Desmond Neill. I should also like to thank L. Braswell, J. Couchman, F.E.L. Priestley, A.G. Rigg, and N. Swerdlow for chairing the sessions; J.N.P. Hume, Master of Massey College, for his entertaining welcome to the members of the conference; and Nancy Rovers-Goheen for setting the text.

Dating Unpublished Notes, Such As Galileo's on Motion
Stillman Drake

At the Central National Library in Florence, bound in volume 72 of the Galilean manuscripts, are 160 folios of notes on the motions of heavy bodies, written between 1602 and 1637. No folio is dated, nor is there any evidence of rational arrangement among them, either in order of composition or by grouping of topics. The material comprises Galileo's working papers used in writing his last book, in which he presented his "new science of motion."[1] That was of crucial importance to the development of early modern physics in the seventeenth century, so the notes are of special interest to historians of science. The absence of dating or even rational arrangement of these notes, coupled with the obvious fact that at least some of Galileo's working papers for the book have not survived, long restricted their value, leaving in dispute some basic questions about Galileo's methods of work and the source of his two fundamental contributions.

About one-quarter of Galileo's *Two New Sciences* was devoted to the law of falling bodies while another quarter dealt with projectile paths. Both topics were treated mathematically, in the form of sequential theorems, as had not been previously done with problems of motion. This form of treatment, as well as the fundamental role of the two chief discoveries announced, made Galileo's physics of interest not only for its own sake, but as it is related to the origin of the scientific revolution and to the character of modern science generally. Three principal views of those relations are debated among historians, and I shall outline those later. In 1969 I commented on them in the light of one document, folio 128, which alone of the notes in volume 72 had been published more than a century earlier and had become a perennial source of controversy.[2] My opinion was that if the debates were to be resolved, further documentary evidence would have to come from Galileo's unpublished notes or from a systematic arrangement and probable dating of the voluminous published working papers.

It is understandable that few attempts had been made to do more than arrange and date a selection of notes regarded as particularly important. The editor-in-chief of the most nearly complete edition of Galileo's works had judged it impossible to date these notes, and scholars do not waste time on projects offering no hope of success commensurate with the efforts required. Yet it may happen that a project supposed impossible on seemingly sound grounds is in fact practicable because of special conditions not known to exist until it is seriously undertaken. That turned out to be the case in the matter of Galileo's notes on motion, and it may well apply to other situations of this kind. I am inclined to think that it must apply in at least some instances of papers important to the history of science that have lain untouched, for reasons based on my own experience.

My phrase "situations of this kind" is intended to designate those in which undated working papers of a particular scientist, relating to a unified subject of investigation, exist in considerable volume, were written over a long period of time, and were followed by his clear and orderly exposition of conclusions ultimately reached. Unless the surviving papers are numerous, the situation will not be analogous to the one on which I base my optimism. Ironically, it is the very fact that Galileo's notes were quite numerous which made scholars disinclined to attempt their arrangement in full. My grounds for optimism, based on several years' experience, had thus seemed grounds for pessimism when the situation was looked at a priori. This may seem paradoxical, but there is a reason, reflected in the adages "you never know till you try" and "God helps those who help themselves."

The key to such situations is one well known to cryptographers; namely, that if the amount of coded material is sufficiently large, any code can be broken in time, though not without effort. By "sufficiently large," they mean in a quantity so great that the probability of more than one consistent decipherment becomes vanishingly small. How large the volume must be depends on the complexity of the code, and that can be determined only by an effort to break it. If no effort is made, there is no telling whether the available material is enough. Cryptographers have standard techniques, which they apply in an established order, to make their efforts as efficient as possible. In the situations to be discussed, we can establish similar procedures.

We are considering material written by a single scientist, which must therefore have been composed sequentially. The code to be broken is random disordering of the material. One thing we know at the outset is that as Galileo viewed what he wrote, each step was based on what he had previously demonstrated. A great many of the notes embody propositions with Euclidean proofs, and we have Galileo's own statement in his previous writings on motion that such a sequence of steps was his goal.[3] We have also various other kinds of available evidence for ordering the notes, to be applied in a certain order of priority if our efforts are to be of maximum efficiency.

Standard editorial techniques for dating manuscript material begin with what may be called "physical evidence." This includes handwriting, ink, and writing material (usually paper when scientific documents are under study). Paper provides various objective clues to its time of use by comparisons among documents with respect to weight, colour, process of manufacture, spacing of chain lines, and often watermarks or countermarks.[4] Next in objectivity after these come the identifiable habits of a given writer during periods of his life in favouring certain words, or abbreviations, or forms of certain letters or ligatures, and so on. Finally, there are kinds of evidence that are more subjective, including the psychological plausibility of a given arrangement, agreement with hypotheses drawn from the material itself or from common habits of writers, and assumptions about philosophical biases, ulterior motives, and societal patterns that may have influenced the scientist in proceeding as he did.

It is generally agreed that priority is to be given to objective evidence, starting with physical clues. Those may seem very limited, but when there is a large volume of material, physical evidence may be present that turns out to be of crucial importance in some way that was not anticipated. In the case of Galileo's notes on motion, it was watermark evidence that broke the back of the problem of arrangement and dating as a result of unusual and accidental circumstances that will be explained later. My present point is that whenever there is voluminous material, I think it probable that *some* kind of physical evidence will serve to establish *some* vital fact on which it would not normally be expected even to throw light. That happened to be watermarks in my project.

In specifying voluminous material as a condition of probable success, I added the requirement that scientific working papers to be arranged and dated shall have led their writer to an orderly presentation of conclusions he reached. It may seem that I said that only because without such evidence that the writer progressed, there would be little point in arranging and dating his steps. The historical incentive for our effort is to discover an order and to identify the steps that were of particular importance to the writer in reaching an integrated understanding of his subject. But I had also another purpose, less obvious, and that was to caution you against a potential waste of time and effort that is most likely to exist when the scientist *did* arrive at new and useful conclusions and then published them in an order that would be clear to any reader.

In such cases there is a strong temptation to work backwards, assuming that all notes relating to advanced propositions came last, and that those relating to elementary matters must have been written first. Experience indicates that such assumptions are more than likely to delay the correct chronological arrangement. Worse still, they may result in a delusive arrangement that lacks support except from a kind of circular reasoning. I shall illustrate this by an example from Galileo's working papers.

Galileo was investigating what were called, from Aristotle's time to his own, "natural motions." By this was meant motions undertaken spontaneously by bodies when merely released from constraint. As Aristotle had observed, such motions are faster at the middle of their duration than at the beginning; that is, natural motions are characteristically accelerated. Now, uniform motions are the easiest to analyze, and Galileo eventually did find a way to reduce accelerated motions to analysis in terms of certain related uniform motions. Having read his *Two New Sciences*, we know that, and hence may be tempted to place Galileo's notes about uniform motion among his first working papers to be written. But with a single exception, which itself is not beyond question, handwriting shows that all the notes setting forth rules of uniform motion were written very late in Galileo's life.

It is easy to understand why that is so. When a writer is ready to present new conclusions to the public, he has to adopt an order of presentation in which they will be most readily understood and accepted by the public. But if Galileo had arrived at his conclusions in that way, it would not have taken him thirty years to do so, or even five. What he may reasonably be expected to have written first would not be something simple, or taken from the writings of earlier scientists, for these were already in Galileo's head and were used by him as a matter of course. The first note to have been saved, destined to become part of a long series of notes, would more probably state some striking new result, supported by only the sketchiest proof, or some conjecture that was not even true. Such propositions arrest a scientist's attention and incline him to write them down with the intention of pursuing further inquiries. If I had realized that when I started in 1972, it would have saved me quite a lot of time.

In short, you should not forget that you know more about the early scientist's subject than he did. Working papers are accumulated and saved because the writer is ignorant and wishes to learn. Galileo began in ignorance of many things we now know, even from reading his *Two New Sciences*, and at no stage of his working papers should he be credited with unevidenced knowledge. The modern historian or editor may know things achieved by earlier writers that Galileo did not know. Also, Galileo may have "known" — that is, may have believed — things now known to be incorrect. When I said we now know more about a subject than did the writer of undated notes on it, I meant only to warn you, in the interest of efficiency, to apply your superior knowledge very sparingly during the investigation. I did not mean to deny that the writer may have known things you do not, including much that you may have to learn while arranging his notes. His methods of work might have been different if he had known all that you do. For example, I know more mathematical techniques than Galileo did, but he knew more about those of Euclidean geometry than I do. Again, his approach to problems of infinite sets and continuity was sound, but it was not our present approach, so I had to learn how Galileo approached them as he found out more and more about accelerated motions.

I am convinced that the most efficient way to start any task of this kind is to postpone as long as possible the adoption of hypotheses based on greater knowledge, not to start from those. Begin with physical evidence, however little there may appear to be, or however scattered it is and tedious to collect. There is always some such evidence, and it pays to exhaust that before scrutinizing the contents of notes carefully for clues to their ordering. This is bound to be the most efficient approach because, in the end, you are not going to escape the trouble of collecting and sifting all available physical evidence anyway. If you do not do that, some other scholar will, and your most treasured conclusion may be refuted later by some neglected evidence from handwriting, ink, watermarks, or other physical evidence.

It follows that throughout the whole investigation, physical evidence should be allowed veto power over hypotheses and assumptions. Negative evidence is not evidence devoid of value. When we start on a jigsaw puzzle, we look first for pieces having one straight side, to construct the border. Nearly every piece is examined at the outset, though most of them must be laid back as not part of the border. If all are laid back, we next suppose the border to be round, or oval, and search again for pieces fitting that hypothesis. It seems a waste of time for us to examine pieces then laid back, a waste that is forced on us by the necessity of doing the border first. But it is not time entirely wasted. Many things noted in the process turn out to be helpful later, as the picture begins to take form. An analogy is casual examination of handwriting in the early stages. It is hard to scrutinize handwriting without reading it, and when the ultimate goal is arrangement, time spent in reading and rereading every note is never wasted. Complete familiarity with content of all notes is the main thing that will be needed toward the end of the task of arranging and dating them, and the best time to start acquiring such familiarity is before any deliberate hypotheses are formed while only physical evidence is being sought.

So much for generalities; let us turn to my particular project. Every edition of a writer's "complete works" necessitates editorial decisions as to the inclusion or exclusion of various papers. Those that have no evident value to scholars who will use the edition would be unduly expensive to transcribe, print, and index. Hence the phrase "complete edition" is always intended not in its literal sense, but in that of selection after conscientious editorial screening with an eye to economic realities and probable scholarly utility.

Such a screening of Galileo's writings was carried out by

Antonio Favaro as editor-in-chief of the *Edizione Nazionale* of Galileo's *Opere*, published in twenty volumes during the years 1890-1910.[5] Favaro, professor of engineering at the University of Padua, was outstandingly qualified for the task. He had already edited and published many manuscripts by or relating to Galileo. Trained in physical science, Favaro was a student of history; he was accomplished in the languages in which Galileo wrote, and he was tireless in the search for scattered documents in archives and collections, both in Italy and abroad. By temperament, Favaro was disinclined to offer conjectures except in prefaces separated from his texts; he confined his textual notes to variant readings in scribal copies and printed versions, or to emendations of readings based on established editorial practices.

A single editorial decision, made in 1898 by this uniquely qualified editor, applying a perfectly reasonable criterion of exclusion at the time, was destined to have consequences that Favaro could not have foreseen. During the present century there has arisen a sharp controversy over the nature of the Scientific Revolution and the character of physical science itself, centering on Galileo's physics. Had Favaro published but one more of Galileo's notes on motion, that controversy would probably not have centered on Galileo, and it might not have arisen at all. Though that must sound incredible to you now, I am quite serious about it. To explain why, I must ask patience from both those of you who are editors and those who are historians of science, since I must speak of matters in either field of expertise that are already familiar to one group but perhaps not to the other.

A train of fortunate accidents preserved nearly all the working papers on motion used by Galileo when writing his last book. Doubtless he would have discarded them when the book was published, but by that time he had become blind and his papers were jealously guarded by Vincenzio Viviani, who had come to study under Galileo in 1638 and served as his secretary until Galileo's death in 1642. Even unlettered diagrams and unidentified calculations were saved by Viviani. Why Galileo himself had preserved such a miscellaneous collection of notes dating back as far as thirty years can be briefly explained.

Motion was Galileo's chief interest from his student days at the University of Pisa to the end of his life. Even the astronomical work for which he is most celebrated centered on the question of motion of the earth. His earliest scientific writings, composed even before his move to Padua in 1592, included a dialogue and a treatise on motions of heavy bodies. Those were coherent, discursive expositions designed for the instruction of others. As a very young man, Galileo believed that he already knew all that was needed to be known about motion in order to correct many errors taught by Aristotle.

The notes with which we are here concerned were begun two decades later and are of a very different kind. These are notes of a man who was learning as he went along, one who was not yet ready to communicate to others what little he truly knew about actual motions of heavy bodies. The thread that links the notes is that of investigation and discovery, in the course of which new knowledge induced Galileo to rephrase and even contradict things he had previously written. The most difficult and most rewarding part of the task of arranging them comes in discerning such new knowledge, identifying its sources, and seeing how such reorientations do not really violate Galileo's rule of making each step depend on what had already been established, though they inevitably must appear to violate consistency from any fixed standpoint whatever.

The earliest notes in volume 72 belong to 1602, on the basis of a dated letter describing Galileo's conclusions late in that year. He soon projected a book on natural motions treated mathematically, and in mid-1609 he was actively at work on it. Just then the advent of the telescope diverted his attention to astronomy. In 1610 he moved to Florence, and not until 1618, after he had been silenced on motion of the earth, did he resume work on his book on motion. Almost at once he was drawn into other controversies, but he filed his notes on motion in marked folders. Two of the cover sheets, themselves bearing later notes and calculations, survive among the

160 folios. Finally, after his trial and condemnation in 1633, Galileo completed and organized his book on natural motions, using notes written as long as thirty years before.

The first attempt to arrange chronologically a large selection of the notes on motion was published in 1895 by Raffaello Caverni.[6] As a historian of science, Caverni assumed that Galileo had started his inquiries by recording results from work done by predecessors; that the order of composition reflected logical progress from such a start; and that it was easy to distinguish important notes and safe to ignore unimportant ones. The results so arrived at by Caverni were entirely misleading. Had he started from handwriting instead of assumptions and logic, he would not have made egregious errors of dating Galileo's two chief discoveries. Caverni dated Galileo's first attempted demonstration of the law of fall to 1622, whereas it can in fact be shown to belong to October 1604 on physical evidence alone, as will be seen presently. What that correction implies is a totally different approach on Galileo's part. Similarly Galileo's first notes on the parabolic paths of projectiles, which belong to 1608–9 on handwriting and watermark evidence, were misassigned by Caverni to Galileo's final years, after 1633.

In 1898 Favaro published a great many more of Galileo's notes on motion, placing some as footnotes to the text of *Two New Sciences* and others in appendices to that text. In his preface to the volume, Favaro stated clearly that many detached notes were not published, referring apparently to those unidentified as to purpose by containing even a single complete sentence. Favaro did not specifically date any individual notes, but he did classify two main forms of handwriting, designating as "youthful" the notes written before Galileo's move to Florence in 1610. Thus Favaro implicitly corrected Caverni's error of supposing the notes on parabolic trajectories to be of late date. Also, by placing Galileo's first attempted demonstration of the law of fall as fourth in order among all the notes published on accelerated motion, Favaro implied for it a date well before 1610, in contrast with Caverni's 1622. In other respects, however, Favaro generally adopted Caverni's ordering, within which he inserted many previously unpublished notes, at places indicated by considerations of handwriting and of topic. As was said before, Favaro expressed the opinion that the surviving notes on motion were far from complete and that they could not be confidently arranged in their order of composition. Both statements, taken in an absolute sense, are correct, but they have served only to retard our understanding of Galileo's physics and its evolution at his hands. To historians of science, the notes of principal interest are those written up to the time at which Galileo had found both the law of fall and the parabolic shape of projectile paths. That was in 1609 at the latest, and the surviving notes up to that year are complete in the ordinary sense of the word. I shall explain later how that fact was established from watermarks, once the border of this jigsaw puzzle had taken form. Completeness makes it possible to arrange the notes through 1609 in probable order of composition with confidence, though of course not beyond any shadow of doubt. The available evidence is of many kinds, each kind forming an independent thread; and though no single thread could bear much load, a fabric woven from all the many threads supports one plausible and consistent ordering of the papers. Any substantial change then reveals internal inconsistencies or implausibilities.

I do not fault Favaro for his omission of unidentified diagrams, calculations, and notes bearing no more than isolated words or abbreviations. Galileo's original notes were, and still are, accessible to any scholar, all at one place, and even bound together. In such circumstances an editorial decision to leave many of them unpublished cannot be blamed. It is, however, a habit of scholars to rely solely on the documents transcribed in a printed edition of "complete works" when one exists, and the tendency to do so is the stronger as the editor was the more highly qualified and reliable.

Three principal theories of Galileo's science and his procedures have found support among scholars who relied on printed editions and did not consult Galileo's original notes on motion; the last theory completely reversed the first. They may be briefly summarized as follows. Nineteenth-century historians of science, mainly trained as scientists, assumed Galileo to have arrived at new conclusions in physics by designing experiments and making careful measurements. In *Two New Sciences* he carefully described the apparatus and procedures used in verifying his law of fall. It was natural to assume that he had discovered the law in much the same way; indeed, no alternative seemed possible, since the times-squared law of natural motion is by no means obvious, nor had it been stated before Galileo's time.

Not long after Favaro's edition of Galileo's works was completed, however, historians discovered that some natural philosophers of the 14th century, engaged in classifying all possible kinds of motion,[7] had defined uniformly accelerated motion and devised a postulate of "middle speed" by which such motion could be compared with uniform motion, of which some rules had been laid down by Aristotle. Medieval writers did not relate this analysis of motion to actual fall of heavy bodies, but it became apparent that they, or anyone after the 14th century, could have done that. Since the times-squared law can be deduced from the medieval definition and postulate, Galileo might so have deduced it, in which event all that had to be granted to him was use of experimental measurement to link a mathematical law with actual descent of heavy bodies. Many historians accordingly partially reversed the earlier view and denied experimentation any role in Galileo's discovery, though not in his linkage of mathematics with physics.

In 1939, without positively asserting that Galileo had reasoned from medieval mean-speed analysis (as it is called), Alexandre Koyré proposed a complete reversal of the original view.[8] Koyré asserted that Galileo's alleged experiments were devised and performed in thought alone, as had been done by all previous writers on motion. The origin of the scientific revolution of the 17th century, Koyré concluded, lay not in a *turn* to direct investigation of nature by painstaking measurement, but in a *re*turn to pure mathematical thinking in the Platonist tradition that disparaged sensory evidence. A decade later, as adherents of this theory of science and its history multiplied, Koyré ridiculed Galileo's published description of his apparatus and procedures as fictitious and even fraudulent, arguing that Galileo could not have achieved results consistent within one-tenth of a pulse-beat, as he claimed.[9] After another decade Thomas B. Settle built the apparatus, followed Galileo's procedures, and reported that twice the disputed accuracy was easily attained.[10] Nevertheless, Koyré's theory of science and its historical origins continued to prevail among eminent historians of science.

The thesis that experiment played no essential role in Galileo's physics, basic to Koyré's theory, is contradicted by a document related to the discovery that projectile paths are parabolic, found among Galileo's notes. That folio, numbered 116 verso, was left unpublished by Favaro. It was the only borderline case if I am correct about Favaro's editorial criterion for exclusion, since by the addition of an obvious verb f 116 v. would contain a single complete sentence.

In 1973 I published this folio which you see as Figure 1A, more legible in the English transcription of it shown in Figure 1B, together with a reconstruction of the experiment suggested by the diagram and of the measurements and calculations made by Galileo.[11] His identification of the unit of measurement as the punto (pū) made complete reconstruction possible, because on f 166r, which Favaro did publish, Galileo drew a line that he described as 180 *puncta* long. Measurement of that line established Galileo's *punto* as 0.94 mm, so that his table of 828 *punti* was 78 cm high, about the same as modern tables. The time of free fall through that height is just under 0.4 second. Computations by modern formulae show that a ball was rolled down a grooved inclined plane from each of the heights shown above the table, losing a percentage of the acceleration for roll on a smooth plane. At the table it was deflected, and after a short horizontal roll the ball fell to the floor. Distances measured by Galileo to the points of impact agree well with those expected by calculation. It is clearly true that Galileo devised and performed actual experiments and made careful measurements.

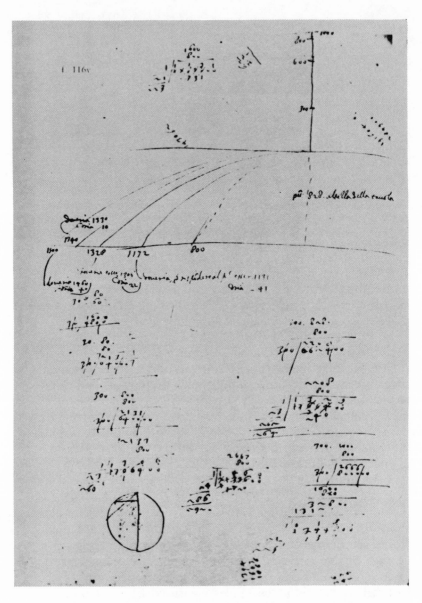

Figure 1A : Galilean mss vol 72, f 116v.

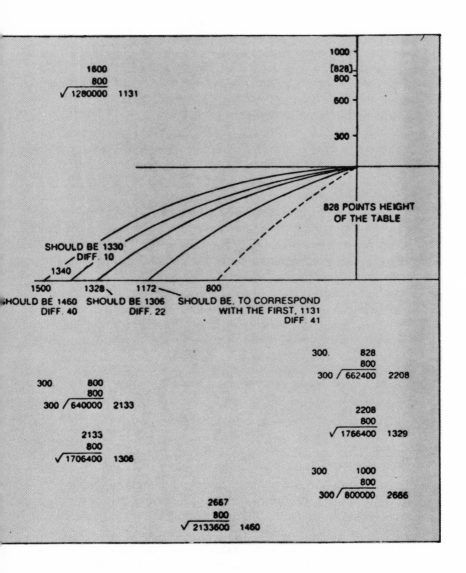

Figure 1B: ENGLISH TRANSCRIPTION of f 116.

In 1898, when Favaro decided to omit f 116v, no historian of science doubted that Galileo had made actual experimental determinations. Since f 116v merely served to confirm what no one then doubted, it is not surprising that Favaro left this document unpublished. Had he transcribed and published it, some historian of the old school would long ago have measured the line on f 166r and reconstructed the experiment of f 116v as I did. In the face of that, historians would have been unlikely to support a theory of Galileo's mentality based on pure Platonism and fraudulent claims of actual measurement.

That f 116v represents also Galileo's discovery of the parabolic trajectory is suggested by curves drawn from the table-top to the floor. Its dating is quite secure. The curves closely resemble a set drawn by Galileo in a dated letter early in February 1609, discussing his recent work and alluding to artillery shots. That letter was written in a crabbed hand associated with rheumatic attacks suffered frequently by Galileo, and so are several of the notes concerning theorems on parabolic trajectories. Most of the working papers on parabolas written at Padua are found on paper bearing a "rhinoceros" watermark, which occurs among Galileo's dated letters only in the years 1607 and 1609. Finally, the proposition which made possible the experiment of f 116v is found at the end of a page of densely written notes that (on other evidence) belong to the latter part of 1607. This illustrates what I meant when I spoke of a fabric of evidence woven from threads of different kinds.

Letters were the primary documents used in dating notes, but by no means the only ones. Most of Galileo's letters are preserved in the same Florentine collection that includes his notes on motion, where there are also other manuscripts for which datings are fairly certain. Watermarks in papers used by Galileo at Padua were found to differ from those in papers he used at Florence, as I had expected. Hence the watermarked notes on motion can for the most part be sorted between those two cities, permitting assignment of dates to them as before or after September 1610. Next, many unwatermarked notes could be similarly sorted, using indications from handwriting. Inks are also useful in this sorting, those used at Padua being non-corrosive and having remained black or grey, whereas inks used at Florence were often corrosive and have turned brown or crystalline. With few exceptions there was little problem about dividing the entries on the 160 folios into those of Paduan and those of Florentine origin. The gigantic jigsaw puzzle thus became two separate puzzles, which happened to be about equal in size. Since Galileo's two main discoveries of interest to historians were made while he was still at Padua, I shall speak only of the notes of Paduan origin. The most common watermark at Padua was a crossbow, found in many sizes and designs. The most frequently occurring countermark was that called "mountains," which also varied considerably in dimensions. These common marks did not produce many exact identities between notes and dated letters. But some infrequent marks did give several secure benchmark dates. Galileo probably bought paper every month or two, usually from the same Paduan stationer, who in turn usually bought from the same supplier. In that way Galileo would have from time to time, but not for long, a supply of watermarked paper agreeing exactly in his notes and dated letters.

The important and controversial f 128, with Galileo's first attempted proof of the law of fall, is connected by theme and by some exact phrases with a letter he wrote to Fra Paolo Sarpi on 16 October 1604. It bears an uncommon countermark that I found elsewhere at Florence only on f 4 of volume 47, a page of notes about a new star that appeared in October 1604. The original letter written to Sarpi is now at Pisa, where I found the same rare mark on its cover sheet, while the letter bore a distinctive ornamented crossbow watermark. At Florence I found this exact mark on only two folios, both of which are bound in volume 47 and bear notes about the new star of October 1604. The date of f 128 is therefore certain. Other benchmark datings of Paduan notes were made from watermark evidence, each of which then permitted a cluster of notes similar in handwriting or content to be

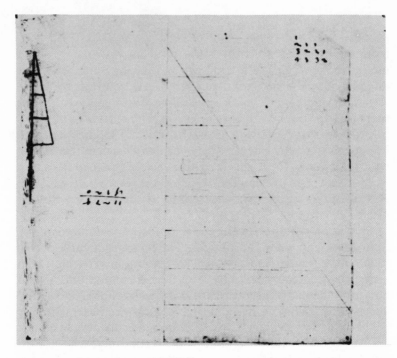

Figure 2: Galilean mss vol 72, f 180v.

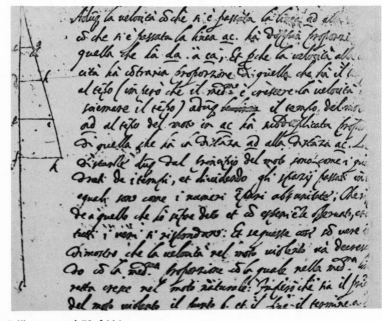

Galilean mss vol 72, f 116v.

approximately dated. This process was rather like assembling the border for a jigsaw puzzle.

Close comparisons of handwriting to judge consecutive or neighbouring entries are difficult to make between the originals, where successive entries may be bound a hundred pages apart. Xerox enlargements were made from a microfilm, from which entries made at differenct times on the same page were cut apart. Such entries are recognizable by ink, handwriting, content, or placement. They were then placed side by side with other folios for comparisons of letters like b, d, and p, habitual ligatures and abbreviations, and other variable habits providing clues to nearness in time of writing. All the separate entries were arranged in loose-leaf binders, one for Paduan notes and one for Florentine.

Other kinds of clues soon began to appear. For example, when Galileo had nearly filled a page, or when he had before him an earlier folio for consultation on some special problem, he sometimes drew a little sketch as an idea occurred to him, and then took a clean sheet and properly ruled and lettered a similar diagram with which the thought was pursued. Several such sketches preceded the writing of f 128, an example of which will illustrate this kind of clue.

On Figure 2, at the top, you see the verso of f 180, a cut page on the recto of which was Galileo's first correct theorem about motions along inclined planes, dating from 1602. He had reason in 1603 to puzzle over this theorem because although he had derived his result without considering acceleration, it held true for actual motion accelerated from rest. In one ink you see a roughly ruled "triangle of speeds" in acceleration, and to the left, in different ink, there is a smaller triangle with the vertical line extended down. Below, you see the beginning of f 128v with the modified triangle drawn and lettered for use in the attempted proof. This diagram occurs elsewhere only on the recto of f 128, where the proof began, and in one closely related Latin demonstration, on f 85. When Galileo thought of the attempted first proof, he had before him the page containing his first correct theorem, and an earlier note about its puzzling feature. This implies a very different origin of Galileo's controversial attempted 1604 proof from the usual conjecture adopted by historians who considered f 128 only in isolation.

Even when grounded in physical evidence, hypotheses like this cannot be proved, but they do fit with common sense and ordinary practices of writers, and do not lead to incongruities in arranging the notes. The essential completeness of the surviving Paduan notes follows from hypotheses grounded in physical evidence. Since essential completeness of Paduan notes was my basis of faith that Galileo's notes could be confidently arranged in order of composition, I shall recount the circumstances, which could not have been foreseen logically.

Among the 160 folios, about one-quarter are not in Galileo's hand. Favaro identified the alien hands as those of two young men who studied with Galileo at Florence after 1614. Most of these folios bear verbatim copies of propositions and proofs from originals that are also present. Though that was a bit puzzling, it at first did not seem important. When classifying and measuring watermarks, however, I noticed that all the watermarked copies bore the same mark, in one of two sizes differing by 3 mm. The two sizes were randomly distributed among the papers used by the two copyists, suggesting that all the copies were made at one place, from a common supply of paper, and over no long period of time. The place would have been Galileo's house, where the originals were kept, but no reason appeared why the period of copying had been the same for two students, or why they had not carried their copies away. Internal evidence suggested the answers.

Nearly always a copy was of a single proposition, written on one side of the page with the other side left blank. There were cases in which both copyists used the same original, on which there were several propositions, but they never both copied the same one. That suggested that the copyists worked under direction from Galileo, who wanted copies for his own use when he returned after several years to the writing of his book on motion. Propositions written on separate sheets could be arranged by him at will, and interleaved with related or with new material. This hypothesis was confirmed when I found that the surviving originals from which copies were made were all of Paduan origin, as already sorted out by watermarks and handwriting. Next, everything of Paduan origin that would be used in a book was found to have been copied, except for a few propositions that were originally on separate sheets. It then followed that in all probability the copies for which the originals are not found were likewise taken from Paduan notes that have not survived. Thus all the Paduan work that Galileo later considered important still exists, either in his own hand or in a copy made at Florence, usually in both forms.

With strong evidence that the Paduan notes are virtually complete, and with several benchmark datings among them established by objective physical evidence, the probability that a single consistent and plausible ordering could be found for them all became very great. Since those are precisely the notes of greatest interest to historians of science, because they include both of Galileo's fundamental contributions to physics, the time and effort required in finding such an ordering no longer mattered. The general criteria employed throughout the project have already been described, and some particular applications have been illustrated. One further illustration seems to me desirable, to show how it may come about that a key document may be misplaced in the early stages because the only clue to its correct placement cannot be recognized, let alone interpreted, until nearly everything else is in place. In this instance I had felt obliged to ascribe to good luck on Galileo's part something that he had found by ingenious and careful work early in his investigations of accelerated motion.

As was seen from f 116v, which led Galileo to the parabolic trajectory, one source of new knowledge for him was careful measurement. Only a few folios unmistakably recorded measurements, and none of them explained in words his experimental procedures. Accordingly I placed them all after f 116, the first evidence I had of such activity, and they remained uninterpreted. Pending further clues to their nature and purposes, I supposed them to have been written at Padua in 1608-9.

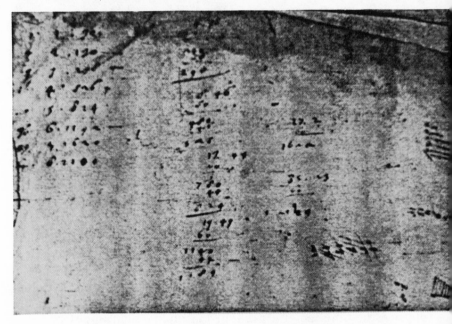

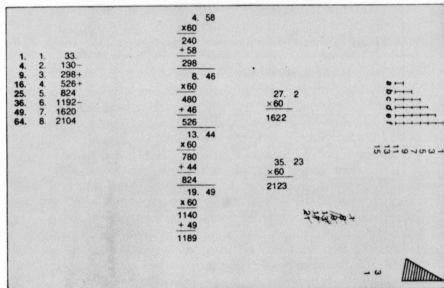

Figure 3 : Galilean mss vol 72, f 107v.

Galileo's first fundamental discovery, the law of fall, had been made several months before October 1604. The event was not clearly explained by the notes around that period, though there were some notes containing conjectures about a rule of speeds in acceleration at the end of 1603, a rule needed for the work then in progress. One of these, f 152r, suggested that a lucky guess from ratios of small numbers in an example had led to the times-squared rule of distances in fall.[12] Eventually, however, I studied the folios recording experimental measurements, and with the aid of the information previously obtained from f 116v I found the key document. There is not a word on it, but a variety of notations make it possible to understand it completely in the light of the lacuna existing among the notes that had been assigned to late 1603 and early 1604.

Figure 3 presents the key document, f 107v, together with a printed transcription, the facsimile reproduction being none too legible. The measurements shown in the third column at upper left are in almost — but not quite — exact agreement with distances of descent along an inclined plane in eight successive equal intervals of time. The notations made at the right, with the page turned sideways, however, were certainly not made as late as 1608, for they are very elementary and Galileo had been using everything suggested by them for at least four years by that time. On the other hand, that little triangle of speeds, and the odd numbers representing relative increases of speed during successive equal time intervals, make very good sense indeed if they were entered early in 1604 and led Galileo directly to his times-squared law of fall. That they did is confirmed by the column of the square numbers from 1 to 64 squeezed in at the extreme upper left, in different ink and after the other two columns had already been written. Reconstruction of the experimental measurements that lay behind the figures in the third column, and explanation of the calculations near the center of the page, is unnecessary here. It suffices to say that when f 107v was moved in my loose-leaf binder from 1608-9 to early 1604, it was seen to fit right after Galileo's fruitless conjectures about possible rules of speeds in natural descent. This key document represents his earliest surviving record of careful measurements related to freely moving heavy bodies. Correctly placed, f 107v reveals also how the notations at the right, though not incorrect, originally misled Galileo about the true relation between speeds and times in naturally accelerated motion, which he did not perceive until four years later.

From this example you may see how it is the fitting in of a given note with others that preceded it and with still others that were to follow it, rather than treatment of selected notes in isolation, that establishes as plausible my chronological ordering and dating of all the separate entries, published in reduced facsimile last year at Florence.[13] If that proves to be of value to historians of science, it is to the patient if tedious labours of manuscript editors over many years and in many fields that I am obliged for the basic techniques necessary in the successful pursuit of projects of this kind. It is my hope that other historians of science will be encouraged to apply them to seemingly chaotic working papers yet undated, and that my sketchily described and meagerly illustrated experiences have contained hints that they will find useful.

NOTES

1. *Discorsi e dimostrazioni matematiche intorno a due nuove scienze* (Leyden, 1638); English translation *Two New Sciences* (Madison, 1974).
2. S. Drake, "Galileo's 1604 Fragment on Falling Bodies," *Brit. Jounal, Hist. of Science, 4* (1969) 340–58.
3. *De motu* (ca 1591), ch 11: "The method that we shall follow in this treatise will be always to make what is said depend on what was said before, and, if possible, never to assume as true that which requires proof. My teachers of mathematics taught me this method." I.E.Drabkin and S. Drake, *Galileo On Mechanics and On Motion* (Madison, 1960) p. 50.
4. On a full sheet of paper there were often two marks, one of which appeared at the center of a page when the sheet was folded twice, and the other near a corner of another page. The latter is called here a *countermark*. Countermarks are found in all the papers Galileo used at Padua,

but in none of those he used at Florence. The watermark identified the maker; the countermark probably indicated the buyer for whom the batch was made.

5. *Opere di Galileo Galilei, Edizione Nazionale* (Florence, 1890-1909); reprinted with additions, 1929-39, 1965, 1968. The project was commissioned by the Italian government after Favaro had demonstrated the inadequacy of the so-called "first complete edition" of the mid-nineteenth century.
6. Raffaello Caverni, *Storia del Metodo Sperimentale in Italia*, vol 4 (Florence, 1895) esp pp 303-8, 328-73.
7. These investigations were entirely abstract and not associated with experiments or actual measurements. The medieval rule for falling bodies was based on a different kind of investigation assuming impetus, also without experiment or measurement.
8. Alexandre Koyré, *Etudes Galiléenes* (Paris, 1939); English trans by John Mepham as *Galileo* [sic] *Studies* (Hassocks, Sussex, 1978).
9. A. Koyré, "An Experiment in Measurement," *Proc. Amer. Phil. Society, 97* (1953) 222-37; repr *Metaphysics and Measurement* (London, 1968) pp 89-117.
10. T.B. Settle, "An Experiment in the History of Science," *Science, 133* (1961) 19-23.
11. S. Drake, "Galileo's Experimental Confirmation of Horizontal Inertia," *Isis, 64* (1973) 84-92.
12. Cf S. Drake, "Galileo's Discovery of the Law of Free Fall." *Scientific American, 228* (May 1973) 84-92.
13. S. Drake, "Galileo's Notes on Motion Arranged ... and Presented in Reduced Facsimile" (Florence, 1979), issued in 1980 as Monograph 3, *Annali dell' Istituto e Museo di Storia della Scienza*.

ACKNOWLEDGEMENTS

Illustrations reproduced by courtesy of Biblioteca Nazionale Centrale, Florence.

Editing Middle English Texts: Needs and Issues
Linda Ehrsam Voigts

An examination of Middle English medical writing requires a definition of Middle English. Historians of the English language traditionally consider 1100 and 1500 the boundaries of the Middle English period.[1] However, for nearly the first three hundred years of this era English was the language of England's conquered people, and it survived in written form primarily in devotional and chronicle writings and in popular literature.[2] That is to say, until the last half of the fourteenth century, written language in England for government, trade, and learning was Latin or French. It is only from 1350 that we can trace what is sometimes called the "triumph of English" in the reappearance of English in legal proceedings, guild records, courtly literature, encyclopedias, religious controversy, as a vehicle for — although not subject of — childhood instruction, and — of course — in medical writings.[3] In the following century, the fifteenth, we find the use of English in government administration.[4] With the exception of this official language, called Chancery Standard, written English during the two centuries is characterized by an imprecision in grammatical forms and orthography, largely because of the lack of formal instruction in the language.[5] It is important, therefore, to remember that the emergence of English vernacular medical writing occurred simultaneously with the emergence of the English vernacular, and the matter of rapid language change is a factor in the consideration of these writings.

When we address the considerable body of Middle English medical writings, we are dealing with material compiled or Englished, or both compiled and Englished from the reign of Richard II (1377) until the Tudor monarchs. For convenience, we can consider the period a century, for the introduction of printing in England in 1476 marks the beginning of a different, and well-documented era.[6] English medical writings during this period are, of course, an aspect of the medical practice of the era, but the scope of this paper does not permit comment on the training, practice, and numbers of English physicians, surgeons, barber-surgeons, and empiric practitioners.[7] It is enough to note that our knowledge of these subjects is far from complete; that documentation on the professional records of these groups — and on foreign physicians in the country — is scanty and often ambiguous; and that the anomalous status of medical study at English universities makes it dangerous to infer anything from our knowledge of Continental learned medicine.[8]

Even apart from the issue of medical practice, it is difficult in 1981 to assess the body of Middle English medical writings, notwithstanding the remarkable efforts of Dorothea Waley Singer and Rossell Hope Robbins. Most Middle English medical writing is prose, and prose, particularly *Fachprosa* (with the possible exception of Trevisa's translation of Bartholomaeus Anglicus), unlike Middle English verse,[9] has been largely ignored. Work, which will occupy years, perhaps even decades, is now underway on a much-needed *Index of Middle English Prose*.[10] In the meantime, access to the hundreds of manuscripts containing Middle English prose in British, American,

Continental European, and Japanese libraries is difficult because it must be done through conventional, often inadequate manuscript catalogues. We are not, however, without guideposts for work with medical texts. Pathfinding work with medieval medical manuscripts in all languages in British libraries was done by Dorothea Waley Singer in the early part of the twentieth century. The raw material for her survey[11] may be consulted in the British Library. There are difficulties in using this material, and it is by no means complete,[12] but the estimate of 1032 medical manuscripts in Middle English from the thirteenth through the fifteenth centuries provides a sense of the scope.

Subsequent study of fifteenth-century texts was conducted by H.S. Bennett,[13] but it is because of Rossell Hope Robbins' pioneering efforts that we have a map of the outlines of what remains largely uncharted territory. In his 1970 "Medical Manuscripts in Middle English," Robbins surveyed the medical texts in more than 350 manuscripts,[14] although he has subsequently suggested that the figure "is surely less than a quarter of the estimated total."[15] Still, Robbins' 25% is likely representative and warrants some provisional generalizations about the kinds of medical writing found in Middle English.

Middle English medical writings can be classified in a number of ways, and each system of classification has its limitations.[16] There is first the distinction I have already mentioned, that of verse and prose. A verse medical text serves a functional, rather than aesthetic, aim; it is a mnemonic device enabling the user to recall bloodletting veins, plague cures, a dietary regimen, the medical capacities or "virtues" of herbs or stones, or to include medical concepts in long question-answer educational verses like *Sidrak and Bokkus*.[17] However, in the whole body of Middle English medicine, verse does not bulk large, and if one looks only at prose, a taxonomy must yet be found. Robbins chose to classify texts by the subject matter — diagnosis, prognosis, or therapeutics,[18] the third category the largest by far. While these categories have some use, they reflect twentieth-century concepts — as does the division between surgery and medicine — and when one addresses bloodletting texts, for example, which deal with a procedure that can be used for diagnosis, prognostics, or treatment for a number of specific disorders, the problems with such a classification become apparent. Furthermore, learned compendia or *compilationes* with continuous chapter numbering — clearly intended to be taken as single reference tools — may well contain prognostic, diagnostic, and therapeutic elements. A good example is the unnoticed long compendium occupying nearly 200 pages at the end of Gonville and Caius College MS. 176/97.[19] The compilation begins with a wisdom prologue concluding that a "tyme of lakkyng of wise fysicians" justifies translating the compendium for a barber, Thomas Plawdon of London. Then follows a twenty-page discussion of the origins of illness, whether malfunctions of the members or of the humors, referring to the *Isagoge* of Ḥunayn ibn Isḥāq, Constantine's *Pantechni*, Galen's *Techni*, and the *Canon* of Avicenna. Following is a further commentary on humors, and a section of some fifty-five pages on urines, citing the encyclopedist Bartholomaeus Anglicus (although the material is not to be found in his encyclopedia) and the medical authorities Isaac Israeli and Giles of Corbeil, as well as a commentary on the latter. A long discourse (69 pages) on fevers, next, apparently draws on Rhazes, Hippocrates, Galen's commentary on the *Aphorisms*, and Walter Agilon. Included in this section is a discussion of a technical difference between Galen and Avicenna on the nature of synochal fever. On the remaining thirty-nine pages are to be found three chapters on simple and compound medicines and seven on ailments of specific members before the text breaks off with a discussion of kidney disease in the middle of the 42nd, apparently last, chapter. Obviously, the classification of a text as diagnostic, prognostic, or therapeutic is of little use in dealing with this sophisticated *compilatio*.

The nature of this long compendium in the Gonville and Caius manuscript suggests another approach to the body of vernacular English medicine before 1500, that is, to classify it in terms of the intended audience — layman, educated physician or surgeon, or village empiric. Indeed, this taxonomy works well for sixteenth-century printed texts,[20] and one can readily call to mind Middle English texts included in laymen's household or professional miscellanies, as the *Liber de diversis medicinis* (an English text in spite of the Latin title) in the Thornton Miscellany[21] or the medical sections in the *Commonplace Book of Robert Reynes of Acle*.[22] Similarly, we know of Middle English manuscripts written for, or at least owned by highly trained physicians,[23] and of the Middle English versions of learned surgical treatises, clearly not for the use of the village healer.[24] In the intermediate range are texts written for or by, or both for and by, local leeches, empirics like John Crophill.[25]

This analysis by audience is an appealing one, but it is severely limited by the evidence provided by manuscript witnesses. There are simply many cases for which we do not have enough information to posit the intended reader or user of a given book, particularly where a manuscript seems to have been commercially produced.[26] Furthermore, the evidence, when it is available, may surprise us. One would not consider the long, learned compendium of university medicine that I have described from Gonville and Caius MS. 176/97 to be a work Englished for a barber-surgeon were it not for the statement at the end of the prologue that the translator, Austin, "schal write sum del of theorike & sum del of pratike þorou þe whiche ȝe schulle þe betir entre into þe worchynge of fisyk in tyme of lakkyng of wise fysicians ... nouȝt to clerkys, but to myn dere gossip thomas plawdon, citiseyn & barbour of london" (p 39). Finally, classification by intended audience could mean splitting different versions of the same text. I earlier alluded to bloodletting texts: Michael McVaugh and I recently completed an edition of a phlebotomy also found in Gonville and Caius MS. 176/97. This Middle English text is an expanded translation of a Latin treatise originating two hundred years earlier, which also circulated in England in a condensed version and in a second, even shorter condensation[27] occurring in one instance in a handbook designed for a medical practitioner with small learning.[28] In addition to the Middle English translation of the full Latin version, there is an independent translation of the least technical Latin version, the shorter of the two condensations.[29] A classification by intended user might well place these two Middle English versions of the text in different categories.

We must then look for still another way to classify Middle English prose medical texts that is free of some of the limitations of other systems. The solution I offer has, to be sure, its own limitations, but it may be closer to the medieval understanding of the texts than other taxonomies. This analysis classifies texts on the basis of their origin — academic medical text or popular remedybook — rather than on a hypothetical audience. In brief, it involves asking if a given text displays an attempt to adhere to a technical, learned source on one hand, or does it fall into the more open, adaptable remedybook tradition of *receptaria* on the other? Admittedly, these two divisions represent poles on a continuum, and some kinds of texts — uroscopic, or the second Englishing of the twice condensed phlebotomy — may well occupy an intermediate position. Nonetheless, these categories are useful because one must approach and edit the texts in one category in a way different from that used for the other sort.

Remedybooks comprise the older and the larger category.[30] A large number of Middle English instances have been published since the mid-nineteenth century. These books were the primary medical texts of the pre-Salernitan era, and a number of Old English instances survive from before the Norman Conquest.[31] All Middle English medical works until the latter part of the fourteenth century fall into this category.[32] The textual traditions of remedy books are difficult to trace because they are characterized by adaptation and accretion. They are, of course, to be found in Latin,[33] but in the fifteenth century they may be even more common in England in English or in polyglot form, where the remedies are variously in Latin, French, and English.[34] See Plates 1 and 2.

These *receptaria* sometimes contain elements of zodiacal computation of prognosis; they often contain uroscopy texts for diagnosis, but they are made up mainly of treatments for ailments — more precisely, treatments for symptoms. The

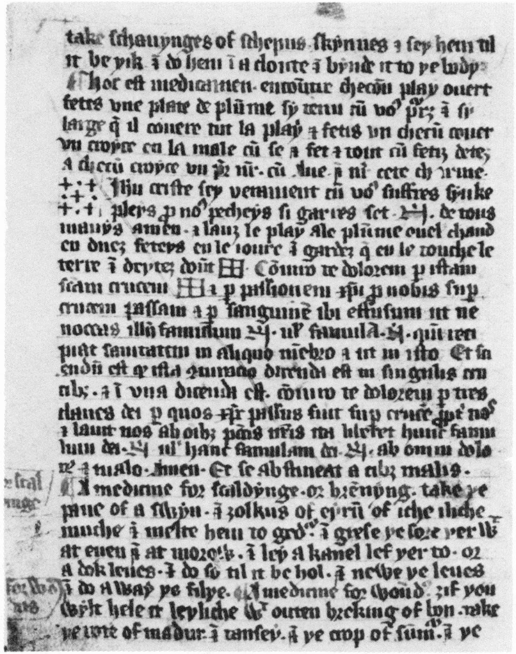

Plate 1. University of Missouri *Fragmenta Manuscripta* No 175r (correctly recto). A leaf from an English remedybook of *c* 1400 illustrating the polyglot nature of such books — note the English, Latin, and French in the first three lines — and the admixture of charms with compound recipes.

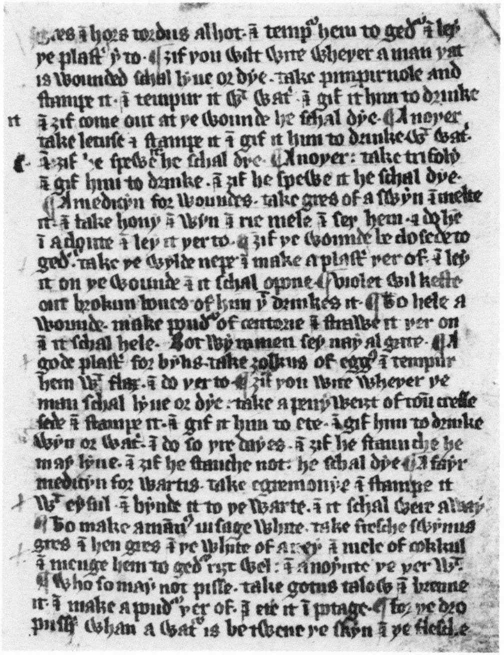

Plate 2. University of Missouri *Fragmenta Manuscripta* No 175r (correctly verso). A leaf from an English remedybook of *c* 1400 illustrating the intermingling of prognostic and therapeutic procedures.

treatments in these practical books may involve minor surgical procedures, non-theoretical phlebotomy, cupping, dietary, charms, prayers, ritual action, and — of course — "prescriptions." These recipes may be simples or they may be compounded from a variety of ingredients — animal, lapidary, or, most often, vegetable. Remedies may be presented in a random order, be organized by ailments from head to foot, or, in the case of herbal simples, by the plant, often in alphabetical order.

To be sure, some collections of herbal simples in Middle English contain botanical information and might be classified as *dynamidia* in the sense used by Isidore of Seville.[35] In this category falls the Middle English *Agnus Castus* with botanical descriptions of 248 plants; there are at least twenty-nine manuscripts of this text which was edited by Brodin.[36] Scores of collections of plant remedies are also to be found where the nature of the material is more fluid and imprecise, as in the Middle English translation of *Macer Floridus de viribus herbarum* edited from eight manuscripts by Frisk, or the related *Here May Men Se the Vertues off Herbes*, edited from three codices by Grymonprez (although Hargreaves deals with forty manuscripts containing the text).[37] It is clear that the plant remedies in many remedybooks derive from the Macer text. Others seem to derive from such collections as the Salernitan *Antidotarium Nicolai*.[38] The variable nature of this kind of collection cannot be too strongly emphasized. Henry Hargreaves' comparison of the variants of a recipe "for clensyng of þe hede," is particularly telling. He presents and discusses the sometimes radically variant forms of that recipe as found in forty codices; he also compares twenty-five recipes for headache and three Middle English compound recipes with seventeenth-century versions.[39]

As one might expect, these variable remedybooks bulk large in the body of Middle English medical texts, and a remarkable amount of editorial energy has been spent on them. Bennett noted forty manuscripts devoted to Middle English remedies in the Sloane Collection at the British Library alone.[40] The largest group of manuscripts catalogued by Robbins falls in this category, and in his search for codices containing the

Middle English prose "Vertues of Herbes," Henry Hargreaves worked with more than 200 remedybooks.[41] The remedybook category is clearly larger than that of academic medical texts, and because a number of remedybooks have been edited, the reader with a limited acquaintance with Middle English medicine is likely to know one or more of the following editions: *A Leechbook ... of the Fifteenth Century*, edited by Dawson; the *Liber de diversis medicinis*, edited by Ogden; *Practica Phisicalia*, edited by Schöffler; *Medical Works of the Fourteenth Century*, edited by Henslow; *Ein mittelenglischen Medizintexten*, edited by Heinrich, and *Aus mittelenglischen Medizintexten*, edited by Müller (and earlier by Stephens).[42] "In Hoote Somere" has received recent editorial attention,[43] and other scholars, like Bühler, Harland, Mayer, and Talbert have described and analyzed other, unedited Middle English texts in the *receptaria* tradition.[44] These Middle English remedybooks will continue to be studied, and indeed, they have much to tell us, but the number of editions may well be disproportionate, given the lack of attention to more learned writings, and the time has come to redress the imbalance in editorial emphasis.

The other, more neglected but quite important, classification is that group of Middle English versions of learned medicine, the writings of antique and Arabic authors and members of the faculties of medicine of medieval universities. Indeed, if the word *academic* can be used in a neutral sense, these texts might be called academic, for they were transmitted or composed in medieval universities. It will be some years before we can claim to have found most of the texts to be studied, but even those that have been identified in manuscript have received little attention. In this category the best known are texts written by surgeons. These texts are called *surgeries* — a label that may mislead inasmuch as the texts usually deal with more than surgery: anatomy; treatment of wounds, fractures, and dislocations; and, frequently, dietary and antidotary material, as well as surgical information. Robert von Fleischhacker published the Middle English surgery of Lanfranc of Milan, presenting readings from two of the eight known codices.[45] Margaret Odgen has edited one version of the *Cyrurgie* of Guy de Chauliac, and Björn Wallner is editing another Middle English translation.[46] One of the works of John Arderne in English, his *Treatise of Fistula in Ano*, was edited by D'Arcy Power.[47] Many Middle English surgeries have escaped any scholarly attention, however. These include the Middle English versions of the other writings of John Arderne, and the surgeries of William of Saliceto, John of St Paul, Roger of Salerno, and Henry of Mondeville.[48]

Other kinds of learned medical writing have received some attention; for example, Beryl Rowland has published an edition of a gynecological work with illustrations of birth positions.[49] Other work has been done on plague treatises, a category that includes texts that fall both in the classification of the remedybook[50] and in that of academic writing, but it is curious that no one has built upon the valuable work done by Sudhoff and Dorothea Waley Singer on Middle English plague texts.[51] A dissertation edition of a Middle English translation of a Gilbertus Anglicus text has recently been completed,[52] but there are still important works from the academic tradition that remain ignored or unknown. Robbins records a treatise on the theory of medicine,[53] and a Middle English version of *De Prognosticatione* of Bernard of Gordon has recently come to light.[54] There is surely a need to study and edit the Middle English versions of the texts listed in Pearl Kibre's "Repertorium of Hippocratic Writings," a catalogue that has appeared in annual installments in *Traditio* since 1975.[55] I have mentioned that Michael McVaugh and I have edited the Latin and two English versions of a theoretical phlebotomy, but other Middle English texts in the same manuscript as the longer version, Gonville and Caius MS. 176/97, badly want editors. One of these is a text already discussed, the long compendium at the end of the manuscript, a combination of texts similar in nature but not in specific content, to the *Articella*.[56] I have not found a Latin equivalent of this text although Luke Demaitre suggests that it may be related to the *Micrologus* of Richardus Anglicus, a work that seems not to have survived in its entirety in Latin.[57] It remains possible that the "Austin" of the prologue was the *compilator* ,as well as the Englisher of the work. In addition to the long compendium at the end of the manuscript, Gonville and Caius MS. 176/97 contains short Middle English texts that warrant editing. On pp 16–19 we find a body of material from the *Isagoge* of Hunayn ibn Ishāq, an introduction to the concepts and doctrines of Galen's *Techni*, in the forms of lists and *quaestiones et responsiones* dealing with the *res naturales*, *res nonnaturales* and *res contra naturam* and providing the categories and subcategories of the *res naturales*: elements, complexions, humors, members, virtues, senses or operations, spirits, and age.[58] See Plate 3. There are other short texts on pages 20 and 21 dealing with the four kinds of causation, with disorders, and with lists of members by complexion.

I hope that the preceding arguments have made a cogent case for employing for Middle English medicine a taxonomy of remedybooks on one hand and learned medicine on the other. I am convinced that further editing of remedybooks is a far less pressing desideratum for Middle English textual scholarship than is the editing of learned treatises, and I shall, for the remainder of this paper, focus on what is to be gained from editorial attention to the academic treatise and to the problems involved in editing the Middle English version of an academic medical text. It is not necessarily patent that editorial activity *per se* is desirable (short of providing graduate students with experience in editing), and the justification for editing these texts must be addressed. When I asked, in a review of the most recent fascicle of Björn Wallner's edition of the Middle English surgery of Guy de Chauliac,[59] whether two editions of Middle English Chauliac texts are desirable — given the number of equally important unedited texts, Nancy Siraisi responded with the apposite query: do we need *any* editions of Middle English medical texts when these texts are translations and there are many important university medical texts in the original Latin for which we have no edition, or no modern edition? To be sure, the absence of Latin editions is much to be regretted, and Nancy Siraisi's question is a fair

one. It deserves an answer, and a number of points should be made in response to it.

The first reason editions of learned Middle English medical texts are needed is that they will give us a clearer understanding of English medicine at the end of the fourteenth century and in the fifteenth century. Again, the state of studies of late medieval English medicine cannot be analyzed here, but it should be noted that English universities were not in metropolitan areas, and that their faculties of medicine did not serve as powerful licensing bodies for medical practitioners as they did at Paris, Montpellier, and the Italian university cities.[60] A phenomenon related to the remoteness of Oxford and Cambridge from population centers is the fact that medicine at the English universities was restricted in its enrollment, often serving as a minor program of study for students pursuing degrees in other faculties, and in many instances the medical degree was only one of several earned by the same individual.[61] Other factors that impede our understanding of late medieval medicine in London include the ebb and flow of political power between the influential guild of barbers on one hand and the less powerful guild of surgeons, sometimes alligned with the physicians in a conjoint college, on the other.[62] In short, there is much to be learned about medical study and practice in England during this period, and one approach that has been little exploited is to examine learned medical writings that survive in Middle English. Latin manuscripts, particularly university texts, cannot always be localized. Academic medical texts found in Continental manuscripts may have been used at Oxford or Cambridge, and many Latin manuscripts now held in English libraries are Continental in origin.[63] In contrast, manuscripts written in the English language provide us *ipso facto* with information as to what texts were read and deemed important during this period in England, and they seem in some instances to provide us with evidence of Latin texts that failed to survive.[64]

A second justification for encouraging editorial work on Middle English academic medical texts has to do with our understanding of the medieval translation processes that became necessary with the growing use of written vernacular languages in Western Europe. Medical writings represent the first substantial body of academic writing to be translated from Latin into English.[65] It is perhaps useful to remember here that the language of theology remained Latin at least until Reginald Pecock in the mid-fifteenth century (consider Wycliff's Latin writings), and it is necessary to wait until the late fifteenth century and Sir John Fortescue for political philosophy, and until an even later period for legal theory in English. On the other hand, medical writing of some intellectual consequence was Englished in considerable quantities from the last quarter of the fourteenth century, and the availability of these texts should enable us to study the medieval vernacular translation of technical writing. For example, it would enable us to measure the applicability of Middle English translation theory as espoused by the revisers of the English Wycliffite Bible — with their methods of resolving the ablative absolute in English — and as articulated by the late fourteenth-century translator John Trevisa.[66] It would also provide us with a body of materials to evaluate in terms of what may have been an Oxford, or at least Queen's College, procedure of translating in two or more stages — a method used by the Wycliffite translators and imputed to that prolific translator of Ranulph Higden and Bartholomaeus Anglicus, John Trevisa.[67]

A substantial body of accessible learned Middle English medicine would also enable us to compare the translation practices used in England with those used for Anglo-Norman and Middle French. The thirteenth century saw some translations into Anglo-Norman of academic surgeries and such Middle French translations of learned medicine as the thirteenth-century translation of Gerard of Cremona's Latin version of the surgery of Albucasis and the 1314 contemporaneous translation of Henry of Mondeville's Latin surgery.[68] Furthermore, a number of studies of French translation practices used for medical writings provide valuable suggestions for study of the corresponding process in England.[69] Similarly, an accessible body of learned Middle English medical prose would allow us to test the generalizations that Middle English translators, and indeed prose writers, worked in isolation and were unaware of one another's activity.[70] The thirteen Middle English versions of the *Secreta secretorum* and half-dozen Englishings of the *De re militarii* of Vegetius have been cited as evidence that Middle English translators were ignorant of one another's work,[71] but that generalization may not be applicable to learned medical prose. We must remember that English medical communities were not large, that the source of the works being translated was, at least ultimately, university medical faculties, and that guilds and licensing provided for professional collegiality. My subjective response to the manuscripts I have seen is that, aside from recopying and condensing, there appears to be less duplication in translation effort than one might think, but that observation can only be tested when a considerable body of medical translation has been edited and studied.

A third and final answer to the legitimate query about the desirability of focusing editorial effort on learned Middle English medicine is that an accessible body of translated *Fachprosa* would enable us to understand more about the development of written English. We should examine the relations of the language of learned medicine to the establishment of Chancery Standard. Can the same regularizing processes Fisher has pointed out for the administrative use of language[72] be seen at work in the translation of medical texts? More important, can we see a relation between the translation of theoretical Latin prose and the expansion of the grammatical capabilities of English during this period? In the fourteenth century English prose had two verb tenses, yet, by 1500 other tenses had been introduced on the model of Latin and independent verbs had been appropriated to serve as modal auxiliaries. Similarly, fourteenth-century prose was essentially paratactic with a high number of coordinating conjunctions and a structure based on repetition, parallelism, balance and contrast, in short, a language quite different from Latin. Yet, by 1500 English had adopted many of the hypotactic capacities of Latin; the fifteenth century saw the introduction of a number of subordinating conjuctions in English and growth of use of a variety of subordinating devices that encourage qualification and signal relationships of cause and doubt.[73] To what degree does the translation of this body of learned technical writing — Latin medicine — illustrate these processes, and to what degree did it affect them?

If it may be granted that editing learned Middle English medical texts is a valid scholarly activity, then it is necessary to address concerns specific to this sort of editing. In an earlier paper in this series of conferences, Anne Hudson skillfully argued the general issues involved in the editing of Middle English, particularly belletristic texts,[74] so it remains only for me to identify those congeries of issues peculiar to the more neglected form of medical writing. The first issue is a simplistic sounding question that must be asked of every learned piece of medical writing: what is the textual unit or units to be considered? Let me illustrate four different applications of this question, acknowledging that there are others — such as prologues — that could equally well be raised. The first three instances arose in editing the phlebotomy treatise I have already mentioned where we have an Englishing of the long Latin version, and another of the shorter of two condensations. To the medieval mind it would likely be havering to question whether these two versions represent the same text, but the modern editor must ask that question.

Another example of the problem of what constitutes a text can be illustrated by the phlebotomy edition. Two short section of the text, one giving general principles for the application of methacentesis and antispasis, and the second discussing the four factors of age, habit, occasion, and strength, can also be found in John Arderne's treatise on phlebotomy[75] and in the Latin *Breviarium Bartholomei* by John of Mirfeld.[76] Neither Arderne nor Mirfeld present the systematic discussion of diseases and appropriate venesection for each disease that makes up the body of the Gonville and Caius MS. 176/97 text, but the resemblance in the two short passages is unmistakable. To what degree should the editor pursue portions of a treatise that circulated independently? Yet another problem is the addition to the end of the Middle English "Of Phlebotomie" of a passage of ca 400 words not to be found in the Latin texts; indeed, some of the Latin manuscripts display different continuations. The addition in the English version cites more recent authorities than the core text and was clearly attached later, but it is so successfully integrated that it appears to be an organic part of the treatise. Surely the fifteenth-century reader did not regard the addition as a separate part. Should the modern editor?

Further instances of the issue of defining a text involve long compendia or *compilationes* where originally independent treatises are preserved in a single treatise with continuous chapter numbering and transitional comment, as, for example, the long *Articella*-like compendium at the end of Gonville and Caius MS. 176/97. Does the Aegidius/Giles of Corbeil material on urines deserve to be treated with other texts where the Giles material is independent? Luke Demaitre has done some important work on Latin medical compendia,[77] and I would argue that the would-be editor of English texts needs to exploit the implications of his study and of the more general work on the theory and practice of *compilatio* of the sort identified with Malcolm Parkes and Alastair Minnis.[78]

A final aspect of the problem of defining a text is the matter of closely related companion texts in Latin and English. An example is a manuscript from the William Norton Bullard Collection at the Countway Library of the Harvard Medical School, MS. 19 in the Ballard *Catalogue*.[79] This codex is an attractive *vade mecum* that A.I. Doyle suspects to be the medical book the scribe William Ebesham copied for John Paston in 1468.[80] In this manuscript the Middle English treatise on urine (14v–19r) is followed by the Latin "Expositiones urinarum in ordine" on 19v–20r. The English "John of Burdews" plague tract follows the Latin text "Tractatus contra morbum epidemialem" on 33r–43r and is identified by Ballard as "a paraphrase and summary of the foregoing tract in English." Furthermore, this vernacular "paraphrase and summary" on 43r–49r is followed by another portion of the Latin version of the tract "Exhortatio bona contra morbum pestilentiam" on 49r–54r. And finally, the treatise on the planets in Middle English is followed by eight leaves containing Latin discussions of astrological signs. An editor must deal with both the Latin and the English texts and must sort out the complex relations among them.

To move from the first congery of issues arising from the question of what constitutes a text to the second of searching for manuscripts and editorial principles is to move from one briar patch to another, but I think the principles in the latter case can be more simply stated. The first principle is that the editor must look for as many manuscripts as possible, considering at least all instances in the Robbins handlist. There are obvious perils in working from only one or two of several manuscripts. The edition of the *Liber de diversis medicinis*, prepared before Robbins' handlist, is based on a single manuscript in the Thornton Miscellany.[81] George R. Keiser has since turned up nine other manuscripts of this Middle English text, and some of them clarify problem readings in the *Liber*.[82]

One should, accordingly, attempt to find all manuscript versions of a text, but it would folly to assume that all *can* be found, given the present state of manuscript catalogues. Perhaps, decades away, with incipit and explicit keys to an *Index of Middle English Prose*, it will be possible to feel confident that one has seen all manuscript witnesses to a text, but that is not the case now. Hence, the present editor must, I think, after searching out all the manuscripts he or she can find (assuming that the text rather than the codex is the focus), simply edit the best of them. A recensionist approach is fraught with problems for any vernacular text, but it is impossible and indeed pointless to use it if there is a likelihood that other manuscripts will turn up after the edition is completed. The best we can hope for now — and in most cases it will be quite good enough — is a good base text edition, perhaps cautiously emended, prepared from the best of the known manuscripts.

The third and final of the large issues to be wrestled with in editing a Middle English learned text is the matter of the Latin text or texts on which the Middle English is based. There may well be no modern edition of the Latin text. That is the case for the *Great Surgery* of Guy de Chauliac; for her edition of the Middle English *Cyrurgie* in Paris, B.N., MS. ang 25, Margaret Ogden selected from the thirty surviving codices of the Latin text four manuscripts to use for comparison, two which seem to be close to the original 1363 text, and two English manuscripts with variants that correspond to the English version.[83] Her procedure illustrates the fact that the search for Latin codices may be as arduous as the search for English manuscripts. The would-be editor fortunately has the resources of the Thorndike and Kibre *Catalogue of Incipits of Mediaeval Scientific Writings in Latin*, and more specialized tools as well.[84] The editor may, however, fail to find a Latin exemplar, a result that is frustrating but makes the edition of a surviving vernacular witness the more important. I would finally suggest that where there is no satisfactory modern edition of the Latin text the editor of the Middle English text would be well advised to coordinate his or her efforts with those of a historian of medicine willing to edit or work with the Latin text. I can say, having had the experience of preparing with a historian of medicine an *en face* edition of the Latin and Middle English versions of the theoretical phlebotomy, that collaboration is invaluable, and that it produces, I hope, an edition with interest for both the student of Latin medicine and the student of Middle English prose.

The inescapable conclusions to be drawn from a consideration of late medieval English medical texts are that there is much work to be done editing Middle English treatises, particularly of the more learned sort, and that there is much to be learned from both the process and the product of those efforts. The vineyard wants workers, and they will be welcome at any hour of the day.

NOTES

1. See, for example, Albert C. Baugh and Thomas Cable, *A History of the English Language*, 3rd ed (Englewood Cliffs: Prentice-Hall, 1978).
2. On English verse from the Conquest to the mid-fourteenth century, see Chs 3, 4, and 5 of Derek Pearsall, *Old English and Middle English Poetry*

(London: Routledge and Kegan Paul, 1977), and, for prose, R.W. Chambers, and his School," in Nicholas Harpsfield, *The Life and Death of Sr. Thomas More*, ed E.V. Hitchcock and Chambers, E.E.T.S. o.s. 186 (London, 1932).

3. Basil Cottle, *The Triumph of English 1350-1400* (New York: Barnes and Noble, 1969), and William Matthews, "Introduction," *Later Medieval English Prose* (New York: Appleton-Century-Crofts, 1963) pp 1-27.

4. Groundbreaking work on this subject has been done by John Hurt Fisher; see his "Chancery and the Emergence of Standard Written English in the Fifteenth Century," *Speculum, 52* (1977), 870-99; "Chancery Standard and Modern Written English," *Journal of the Society of Archivists, 6* (1979), 3: 136-44; and forthcoming book. See also Malcolm Richardson, "Henry V, the English Chancery, and Chancery English," *Speculum, 55* (1980), 726-50.

5. On the implications for English of the absence of formal instruction in the language, see Norman Blake, *The English Language in Medieval Literature* (London: Dent, 1977), esp. pp 51 and 168.

6. A valuable aid for the later period is H.S. Bennett, *English Books and Readers 1475 to 1557*, 2nd ed (Cambridge: Cambridge University Press, 1970), and for medical writings specifically, Paul Slack, "Mirrors of Health and Treasures of Poor Men: The Uses of the Vernacular Medical Literature of Tudor England," in *Health, Medicine and Mortality in the Sixteenth Century*, ed Charles Webster (Cambridge: Cambridge University Press, 1979) pp 237-73.

7. There are a number of works that can be consulted on medical practice. Charles H. Talbot, *Medicine in Medieval England* (London: Oldbourne, 1967), provides an overview, but its use is limited for the serious student because it lacks documentation. On earlier periods, see Stanley Rubin, *Medieval English Medicine* (New York: Barnes and Noble, 1974), and Edward J. Kealey, *Medieval Medicus: A Social History of Anglo-Norman Medicine* (Baltimore: Johns Hopkins University Press, 1981), and for the following era, Margaret Pelling and Charles Webster, "Medical Practitioners," pp 165-235, in *Health, Medicine and Mortality in the Sixteenth Century*.

More specific focuses are to be found in Huling E. Ussery, *Chaucer's Physician: Medicine and Literature in Fourteenth-Century England*, Tulane Studies in English 19 (New Orleans, 1971); D'Arcy Power, "English Medicine and Surgery in the Fourteenth Century," in *Selected Writings* (Oxford: Clarendon, 1931), pp 29-47; George E. Gask, "The Medical Staff of King Edward the Third," and "The Medical Services of Henry the Fifth's Campaign of the Somme in 1415," in *Essays in the History of Medicine* (London: Butterworth, 1950), pp 77-93, 94-102.

A valuable source of information on particular figures is Charles H. Talbot and E.A. Hammond, *The Medical Practitioners in Medieval England: A Biographical Register* (London: Wellcome, 1965).

8. I have discussed these issues *vis-à-vis* vernacular learned medicine in the "Introduction" to Voigts and Michael R. McVaugh, *A Latin Technical Phlebotomy and Its Middle English Translation* (forthcoming). See also below, notes 60–2.

9. The basic reference guide to verse, by first lines, is *The Index of Middle English Verse* by Carleton Brown and Rossell Hope Robbins (New York The Index Society, 1943) and *Supplement* by Rossell Hope Robbins and John L. Cutler (Lexington, Kentucky: University of Kentucky Press, 1965), hereafter cited as *IMEV* and *IMEV Suppl.*

10. See Robbins, "Opening Remarks," pp 3–21; A.S.G. Edwards, "Towards an *Index of Middle English Prose*," pp 23–41; and Robert E. Lewis, "Editorial Technique in the *Index of Middle English Prose*," pp 43–64, in *Middle English Prose: Essays on Bibliographical Problems*, ed A.S.G. Edwards and Derek Pearsall (New York: Garland, 1981).

11. For a brief summary of Mrs. Singer's survey, see her "Survey of Medical Manuscripts in the British Isles Dating before the Sixteenth Century," *Proceedings of the Royal Soc. of Med.*, Hist. of Med. Section, *12* (1918–19), 96–107.

12. See two articles by Robbins, "A Note on the Singer Survey of Medical Manuscripts in the British Isles," *Chaucer Review, 4* (1970), 66–70; and "The Physician's Authorities," pp 335–41, in *Studies in Language and Literature in Honour of Margaret Schlauch*, ed Mieczyslaw Brahmer et al, (Warsaw: Polish Scientific Publishers, 1966).

13. "Science and Information in English Writings of the Fifteenth Century," *Mod. Lang. Rev.,39* (1944), 1–8.

14. *Speculum, 45*, 393–415.

15. "Forward," to Beryl Rowland, *Medieval Woman's Guide to Health* (Kent, Ohio: Kent State University Press, 1981), p xii.

16. On categories in *Fachliteratur*, see William C. Crossgrove, "The Forms of Medieval Technical Literature: Some Suggestions for Further Work," *Jahrbuch für Internationale Germanistik, 3* (1971), 13–21.

17. The bloodletting poem in couplets, "Veynes þer be XXX[ti] and two," is *IMEV* and *IMEV Suppl.* 3848. The *Suppl.* lists twenty-seven manuscripts, four of which have been printed. Perhaps the best known of the printed versions is the one based on Nat. Lib. of Medicine *MS.* 4, ff. 16r–17r; see Claudius F. Mayer, "A Medieval English Leechbook and its 14th-Century Poem on Bloodletting," *Bul. Hist. Med., 7* (1939), 381–91. A plague poem has been edited by R.H. Bower, "A Middle English Mneumonic Plague Tract," *Southern Folklore Quarterly, 20* (1959), 118–25.

John Lydgate's "Dietary," also found in Nat. Lib. of Medicine MS. 4, ff. 64r-64v, was quite popular; *IMEV* and *IMEV Suppl.* list 51 manuscripts and three early printed editions, as well as numerous modern editions, for 824, a poem of ten eight-line stanzas. For one version of the verse "Virtues of Herbs," see *IMEV Suppl.* 417.8, and for another, Arne Zettersten's edition, *The Virtues of Herbs in the Loscombe Manuscript*, Acta Universitatis Lundensis, Sec. 1, Theologica Juridica Humaniora 5 (Lund, 1976). See also Robert M. Garrett, "Middle English Rimed Medical Treatise," *Anglia, 34* (1911), 163–93. Similarly, for the "virtues" of a stone "lapis hematitis," see D.C. Bain, "A Note on an English Manuscript Receipt Book," *Bul. Hist. Med., 8* (1940), 1246–48. Concepts of physiology and disease, as well as specific recipes, are to be found in question-answer form in verse; see Robert E. Nichols, Jr., "Medical Lore from *Sidrak and Bokkus*: A Miscellany in Middle English Verse," *Jnl. Hist. Med., 23* (1968), 167–72.

18. "Medical Manuscripts," p 395.

19. See Montague Rhodes James, *A Descriptive Catalogue of the Manuscripts in the Library of Gonville and Caius College*, Vol 1 (Cambridge: Cambridge University Press, 1907), pp 201–3. This manuscript, to be discussed further in this paper, is analyzed in detail in Voigts and McVaugh, *A Latin Technical Phlebotomy*.

20. Paul Slack, "Mirrors of Health and Treasures of Poor Men: The Uses of the Vernacular Medical Literature of Tudor England," pp 237–73, of *Health, Medicine and Mortality in the Sixteenth Century*.

21. Ed Margaret S. Ogden, E.E.T.S. o.s. 207 (rev. rpt., London, 1969).

22. Ed Cameron Louis, Garland Medieval Texts 1 (New York, 1980).

23. Robbins, "Medical Manuscripts," lists six manuscripts, some containing French and/or Latin as well as English, that were in the possession of graduate physicians (p 408).

24. Bennett, "Science," p 4, and Robbins, "Medical Manuscripts," p 406, name Middle English translations of the surgeries of Lanfranc of Milan, William of Saliceto, John of St Paul, John Arderne, Guy de Chauliac, and Roger of Salerno. In addition to these listings, there are manuscripts containing Middle English versions of the surgery of Henry of Mondeville (e.g., Cambridge, Peterhouse MS. 118, and London, Wellcome MS. 564).

25. The famous Crophill holograph, Brit. Lib. Harley MS. 1735, ff. 28r-52v, is discussed by Ernest William Talbert, "The Notebook of a Fifteenth-Century Practicing Physician," *Texas Studies in English, 21* (1942), 5–30; Talbot, *Medicine*, pp 190–1; James K. Mustain, "A Rural Medical Practitioner in Fifteenth-Century England," *Bul. Hist. Med., 46* (1972), 469–76. It contains vernacular texts in prose and verse on the complexions and elements, bloodletting, uroscopy, diet, days for treatment, and the

like. It also contains miscellaneous recipes and personal notes on the medical practice of Crophill, a bailiff and a rural empiric practitioner who may have received some training as a lay assistant at an Augustinian house.

26. Robbins, "Medical Manuscripts," argues that "it appears very likely that collections of medical recipes were written in commercial scriptoria for speculative sale" (p 413).

27. From a preliminary search Michael McVaugh identified thirty copies of the Latin text — assigned variously to Henry of Winchester, Maurus of Salerno, Richardus Anglicus, Walter of Agilon, Galenus Secundus Salernitanus, and Roger of Salerno. An edition, based on two somewhat debased texts 3066, ff 5v-7v. A condensed version, exemplified by Cambridge, Trinity College MS. was prepared by Rudolf Buerschaper, *Ein bisher unbekannter Aderlasstraktat des Salernitaner Arztes Maurus: "De Flebotomia"* (Inaug.-Diss., Leipzig, 1919). Voigts and McVaugh, *A Latin Technical Phlebotomy*, use as a base text Madrid, Biblioteca Nacional MS. 500, ff 5r-6v, beginning "Minutio alia ..." (the full versions begin "Propositum est ..." or "Presentis negotii ..."), is to be found in five manuscripts in British libraries. There is a second, shorter version that condenses the first abbreviation; it is exemplified by Cambridge, Trinity College MS. 1081, ff 15v-16r.

28. Another, corrupted text of the shorter of the two Latin condensations is contained in the privately owned Dickson Wright MS. 1; it was published by Charles H. Talbot, "A Mediaeval Physician's Vade Mecum," *Jnl. Hist. Med.*, 16 (1961), 223-24. Talbot was unaware of the better, closely related Trinity College MS. 1081.

29. Cambridge, Gonville and Caius College MS. 84/166, pp 205-6, edited as Appendix A in Voigts and McVaugh, *A Latin Technical Phlebotomy*.

30. See John Riddle, "Theory and Practice in Medieval Medicine," *Viator, 5* (1974), 157-84.

31. Linda E. Voigts, "Anglo-Saxon Plant Remedies and the Anglo-Saxons," *Isis, 70* (1979), 250-68.

32. John E. Wells, *A Manual of the Writings in Middle English 1050-1400* (New Haven: Yale University Press, 1916) pp 428-30. While this listing is incomplete, it makes clear the remedybook nature of most medical manuscripts before 1400; only two entries are not remedybooks, and they are the Middle English Lanfranc and John Arderne, both of which were translated near the end of the fourteenth century. Talbot, *Medicine*, p 188, associates many of these books with friars.

33. Ready examples are the manuscripts cited above (notes 27 and 28) containing the second condensation of the phlebotomy treatise. A late fourteenth-century English example of an elaborate and rather sophisti-

cated Latin remedybook was compiled by John of Mirfield, a clergyman at St Bartholomew's hospital who claimed no medical training. Titled the *Breviarium Bartholomei*, it is a compendious work organized by general diseases and then disorders from head to foot. See the request that the reader/user improve the book in the "Proemium," p 48 of the partial edition, *Johannes de Mirfeld of St. Bartholomew's, Smithfield: His Life and Works*, ed and trans by Percival Horton-Smith Hartley and Harold R. Aldridge (Cambridge: Cambridge University Press, 1936). This compendium is mentioned by Luke Demaitre in his discussion of Latin practical compendia written by university teachers, "Scholasticism in Compendia of Practical Medicine, 1250–1450," *Manuscripta, 10* (1976), 81–95, but it surely falls in the more general category.

34. A typical example is a late fourteenth-century instance, Columbia, Missouri, University of Missouri *Fragmenta Manuscripta*, No. 175. In the first three lines of the verso (correctly recto) of this leaf the text changes from Middle English to Latin and then to Anglo-Norman. An example, discussed below (see notes 79–80), of a manuscript containing closely related texts in both Latin and English – dealing with uroscopy, plague remedies, and the planets – is MS. 19 in the Bullard collection at the Harvard Medical School.

35. See Loren C. MacKinney, " 'Dynamidia' in Medieval Medical Literature," *Isis, 24* (1936), 400–14, esp p 401.

36. *Agnus Castus: A Middle English Herbal Reconstructed from Various Manuscripts*, ed Gösta Brodin, Essays and Studies on English Language and Literature 6 (Uppsala, 1950).

37. The 2,269 hexameter-line Latin poem variously titled *De virtutibus herbarum* or *De viribus herbarum* and attributed to "Macer" was probably written by Odo of Meung in the first half of the eleventh century. See *Macer Floridus de viribus herbarum*, ed Ludwig Choulant (Leipzig: Vossius, 1832), and Bruce P. Flood, Jr, "The Medieval Herbal Tradition of Macer Floridus," *Pharmacy in History, 18* (1976), 62–6. An English prose version that is relarively close to the Latin is *A Middle English Translation of Macer Floridus de virivus herbarum*, ed Gösta Frisk (Uppsala: Almquist, 1949). A prose version more loosely based on the Latin is *"Here Men May Se the Vertues off Herbes,"* ed Pol Grymonprez, Scripta 3 (Brussels, 1981). See also Henry Hargreaves, "Some Problems in Indexing Middle English Recipes," in *Middle English Prose*, pp 91–113; and on the Middle English verse versions, see above, note 17.

38. To our knowledge, no one has attempted to sort out the impact of this influential pharmacological treatise on Middle English remedybooks; Bain, "A Note on an English Manuscript Receipt Book," p 1247 (op

cit, n. 17), points out a fifteenth-century English recipe from the *Antidotarium*, and Margaret S. Ogden notes that a number of preparations from it are to be found in the *Liber de diversis medicinis*, p xxiii. For a facsimile of an early printed edition of the *Antidotarium Nicolai*, see Dietlinde Goltz, *Mittelalterliche Pharmazie und Medizin*, Veröffentlichungen der Internationalen Gesellschaft für Pharmazie e. V., n.f. 44 (Stuttgart, 1976).

39. "Some Problems in Indexing Middle English Recipes," pp 91-113.

40. "Science," p 3. This collection should not, however, be considered representative, given the medical interests of Sir Hans Sloane.

41. Robbins, "Medical Manuscripts," pp 400-1, 403-6; and Hargreaves, "Some Problems in Indexing Middle English Recipes," p 91.

42. *A Leechbook or Collection of Medical Recipes of the Fifteenth Century*, ed Warren R. Dawson (London: Macmillan, 1934); *Liber de diversis medicinis*, ed Margaret S. Ogden, op cit, note 21; Herbert Schöffler, *Beiträge zur mittelenglischen Medizinliteratur*, Sächsische Forschungsinstitut in Leipzig 3, Anglistische Abteilung 1 (Halle, 1919); *Medical Works of the Fourteenth Century*, ed George Henslow (London: Chapman and Hall, 1899), *Ein mittelenglisches Medizinbuch*, ed Fritz Heinrich (Halle: Niemeyer, 1896); *Aus mittelenglischen Medizintexten: Die Prosarezept des Stockholmer Miszellankodex x. 90*, ed Gottfried Müller, Kölner Anglistische Arbeiten 10 (Leipzig, 1929); some of the prose remedies in this manuscript were also edited by George Stephens, "Extracts in Prose and Verse from an Old English Medical Manuscript preserved in the Royal Library at Stockholm," *Archaeologia, 30* (1844), 349-418.

43. Elaine M. Miller, " 'In Hoote Somere': A Fifteenth-Century Medical Manuscript" (Ph.D. diss., Princeton University, 1979).

44. Curt Bühler, "A Middle English Medical Manuscript from Norwich," pp 285-98 in *Studies in Medieval Literature in Honor of Professor Albert Croll Baugh*, ed MacEdward Leach (Philadelphia: University of Pennsylvania Press, 1961); J. Harland, "Some Account of a Curious Astronomical, Astrological and Medical Manuscript in the Chetham Library, Manchester," *Transactions, Hist. Soc. fof Lancashire and Cheshire*, Session 29, 3rd series, 5 (1876-77), 1-8; Claudius F. Mayer, op cit, note 17; and Ernest W. Talbert, op cit, note 25.

45. *Lanfrank's "Science of Cirurgie,"* ed Robert von Fleischhacker, E.E.T.S. o.s. 102 (Oxford, 1894), is based on two manuscripts. Robbins, "Medical Manuscripts," p 406, lists six other codices.

46. Robbins, "Medical Manuscripts," p 406, cites seven manuscripts for the Middle English surgery of Guy de Chauliac. Paris, B.N. MS. ang 25 has been edited by Margaret Ogden, *The Cyrurgie of Guy de Chauliac,*

E.E.T.S. o.s. 265 (London, 1971), and New York Academy of Medicine MS. 12 has been edited by Björn Wallner, *The Middle English Translation of Guy de Chauliac's Anatomy, With Guy's Essay on the History of Medicine*, Lunds Universitets Aarsskrift, n.f. Adv. 1, Bd. 56, Nr. 5 (Lund, 1964); *The Middle English Translation of Guy de Chauliac's Treatise on Fractures and Dislocations*, Acta Universitatis Lundensis. Sectio 1. Theologica Juridica Humaniora 11 (Lund, 1969); *A Middle English Version of the Introduction to Guy de Chauliac's Chirurgia Magna*, Acta Universitatis Lundensis. Sectio 1. Theologica Juridica Humaniora 12 (Lund, 1970); *The Middle English Translation of Guy de Chauliac's Treatise on Wounds, Part 1: Text*, Acta Universitatis Lundensis. Sectio 1. Theologica Juridica Humaniora 23 (Lund, 1976); *The Middle English Translation of Guy de Chauliac's Treatise on Wounds, Part II*, Acta Universitatis Lundensis, Sectio 1. Theologica Juridica Humaniora 28 (Stockholm, 1979).

47. Robbins, "Medical Manuscripts," p 406, lists eleven manuscripts containing the Middle English version of John Arderne's *Treatise of Fistula* (p 406); see *Treatises of Fistula in Ano, Haemorrhoids, and Clysters*, ed D'Arcy Power, E.E.T.S. o.s. 139 (London, 1910).

48. See above, note 24. Richard Grothé of the Université de Montréal reports that his work on an edition of the Middle English surgical writings in Wellcome MS. 564 is near completion.

49. *Medieval Woman's Guide to Health*, op cit, note 15.

50. For example, the shorter of the two treatises attributed to John of Burdews/Burgundy is found in the *Liber de diversis medicinis*. See the Ogden edition, pp xxiv, 51–4.

51. Karl Sudhoff, "Pestschriften aus den ersten 150 Jahren nach der Epidemie des 'schwarzen Todes' 1348," (Sudhoffs) *Archiv für Geschichte der Medizin*, 5 (1911), 36–87; and Dorothea Waley Singer and Annie Anderson, *Catalogue of Latin and Vernacular Plague Tracts in Great Britain and Eire in Manuscripts Written before the Sixteenth Century* (London: Heinemann Medical Books, 1950); see also Robbins, "Medical Manuscripts," p 407.

52. Faye Marie Getz, "An Edition of the Middle English Gilbertus Anglicus found in Wellcome MS. 537" (Ph.D. diss., University of Toronto, 1981).

53. Glasgow, Hunterian MS. 307, "Medical Manuscripts," p 399, n 15; this 166-folio treatise is dated late fourteenth century.

54. Bernard of Gordon's *De prognosticatione* in Middle English is to be found in a manuscript recently acquired by Dr Toshiyuki Takamiya; I am grateful to Dr Takamiya for this information.

55. *31* (1975), 99–126; *32* (1976), 257–92; *33* (1977), 253–95; *34* (1978), 193–266; *35* (1979), 273–302. See also her 'Hippocratic Writings in the

Middle Ages," *Bul. Hist. Med., 18* (1945) 371–412.

56. The *Articella*, or *Ars medicine*, a twelfth-century compendium of Salernitan origin, was the basic text for medieval medical study. It contained the *Isagoge* of Hunayn ibn Ishāq (Johannitius), the *Techni* of Galen, a number of Hippocratic writings, and short works on pulse and urines. It can be consulted in early printed editions, for example, Venice, 1483. See Talbot, *Medicine*, pp 42–4.

57. I am most grateful to Luke Demaitre for his suggestions. Texts associated with the *Micrologus* can be considered via Lynn Thorndike and Pearl Kibre, *A Catalogue of Incipits of Mediaeval Scientific Writings in Latin*, rev ed (Cambridge, Mass.: Mediaeval Academy of America, 1963).

58. The Middle Ages, of course, conceived of the *Isagoge* of Hunayn as a Latin work. For a modern translation of the Arabic text, see *Questions of Medicine for Scholars*, trans Paul Ghalioungui (Cairo: Al Ahram Center for Scientific Translation, 1980).

59. Forthcoming in *Speculum*.

60. There are a number of useful studies on this subject by Vern L. Bullough; see "Medical Study at Mediaeval Oxford," *Speculum, 36* (1961), 600–12; and "Population and the Study and Practice of Medieval Medicine," *Bul. Hist. Med., 36* (1962), 62–9. On the licensing role of the Faculty of Medicine at Oxford, see *Munimenta academica*, ed Henry Anstey, Rolls Series 50 (London, 1868), Vol 1, 236–7, and on the greater scope of the Paris Faculty, Pearl Kibre, "The Faculty of Medicine at Paris, Charlatanism, and Unlicensed Medical Practices in the Later Middle Ages," *Bul. Hist. Med., 27* (1953), 1–20.

61. See Bullough, "Medical Study," pp 603–4, "Population," p 69, and *The Development of Medicine as a Profession* (New York: Hafner, 1966), pp 80–1.

62. To study surgeons or barber-surgeons in England one must consult the earliest surviving records of the two crafts assembled in the following volumes: *The Annals of the Barber-Surgeons of London, Compiled from Their Records and Other Sources*, by Sidney Young (London: Blades, East, and Blades, 1890); and *Memorials of the Craft of Surgery in England*, from materials compiled by John Flint South, ed D'Arcy Power (London: Cassell, 1886). These records must be used with care, however. The disposition of petitions recorded in them is not always clear.

63. For example, many manuscripts in the Harley collection at the British Library, particularly those acquired by Edward Harley, the Second Earl of Oxford (1689–1741), are Continental. An interesting instance of a German compilation of learned medical texts acquired for Edward Harley by Nathaniel Noel, a principal supplier of Continental codices, is

Harley MS 4986. See Cyril Ernest Wright, *Fontes Harleiani* (London: British Museum, 1972), pp xv–xviii, 253, and 451.

64. Michael McVaugh and I have not found the Latin text from which the continuation of the phlebotomy in Gonville and Caius MS. 176/97 was Englished. Presumably it began "Notandum quod secundum quosdam ..."

65. To be sure, other kinds of technical and technological writings were Englished. Two well-known examples are Chaucer's translation of the "Tretys of the Astrelabie" (*The Works of Geoffrey Chaucer*, 2nd ed, ed F.N. Robinson [Boston: Houghton Mifflin, 1957], pp 545–63), and Thomas Norton's *Ordinal of Alchemy* (ed John Reidy, E.E.T.S. O.S. 272 [London, 1975]). In comparison with medical writings, however, other scientific texts in Middle English do not bulk large.

66. Chapter 15 of the "Prologue" to the second recension of the Wycliffite *Bible*, the "Dialogue between a Lord and a Clerk upon Translation" from John Trevisa's translation of Higden's *Polychronicon*, and "The Epistle of Sir John Trevisa, Chaplain unto Lord Thomas of Barkley, upon the Translation of Polychronicon into our English Tongue" can all be consulted in Alfred W. Pollard's *Fifteenth Century Prose and Verse* (Westminster: Archibald Constable, 1903), pp 193–210. Another interesting Middle English discussion of problems faced by the translator, in this case Englishing a French text, is to be found in a Middle English Augustinian devotional treatise, Cambridge, Massachusetts, Harvard University, Houghton Library, Richardson MS. 22, f 51. This treatise is being edited by Robert Sturges.

67. On the possible connections between the two or more stage translation procedures used by Wycliffite translators and John Trevisa's methods, see Sven Fristedt, *The Wycliffe Bible: Part III*, Stockholm Studies in English 28 (Stockholm, 1973) pp 8–58, and three articles by D.C. Fowler, "John Trevisa and the English Bible," *Modern Philology, 58* (1960), 81–98; "New Light on John Trevisa," *Traditio, 18* (1962), 289–317; and "More Light about John Trevisa," *Mod. Lang. Quarterly, 32* (1971), 243–64.

68. For a partial listing of Anglo-Norman translations of medical treatises, see Johan Vising, *Anglo-Norman Language and Literature* (London: Oxford University Press, 1923), p 68. Extracts from a number of these translations, including the "Surgical Treatise of Roger of Parma," were published by Paul Meyer in *Romania, 32* (1903), 75–113; *35* (1906), 518; *37* (1908), 510. On Continental French translations, see Howard Stone, "Puzzling Translations in the Thirteenth Century Multiple Equivalents in Early French Medical Terminology," *Romance Notes, 10* (1968), 174–79, and Janis Pallister, "Fifteenth-Century Surgery in France: Contributions to Language and Literature," *Fifteenth-Century Studies, 3* (1980), 147–53.

69. In addition to the study by Howard Stone cited above, see also his "Cushioned Loan Words," *Word, 9* (1953), 12–15; "Learned By-Forms in Middle-French Medical Terminology," *Lingua, 4* (1954), 81–8; and "The French Language in Renaissance Medicine," *Bibliothèque d'Humanisme et Renaissance, 15* (1953), 315–46. See also Guy Beaujoan, "Fautes et Obscurités dans les Traductions médicales du moyen âge," *Revue de Synthèse, 89* (1968), 145–52. We must hope for more scholarly attention to Anglo-Norman texts in the future.

70. The observation that translators outside the monastic/devotional tradition worked in ignorance of one another is a commonplace. See, for example, Matthews, "Introduction," op cit, note 3, pp 5–6; Blake, *The English Language*, op cit, note 5, p 18 et passim; and Samuel K. Workman, *Fifteenth Century Translation as an Influence on English Prose*, Princeton Studies in English 18 (Princeton, 1940), Chapter 3, "Translated Prose: The Quantity and the Provenance," et passim.

71. See Matthews, p 6. *Secretum Secretorum: Nine English Versions*, ed M. A. Manzalaoui, E.E.T.S. o.s. 276 (Oxford, 1977); Henry N. MacCracken, "Vegetius in English," in *Anniversary Papers by Colleagues and Pupils of George Lyman Kittredge* (Boston: Ginn, 1913), pp 389–403; and Charles T. Shrader, "A Handlist of Extant Manuscripts Containing the *De re militari* of Flavius Vegetius Renatus," *Scriptorium, 33* (1979), 302–4.

72. See above, note 4.

73. Blake, *The English Language*, esp Ch 8, "Syntax," and Workman, *Fifteenth Century Translation*.

74. "Middle English," *Editing Medieval Texts: English, French, and Latin Written in England*, Papers given at the twelfth annual Conference on Editorial Problems, University of Toronto, 5–6 November 1976, ed A.G. Rigg (New York: Garland, 1977) pp 34–57.

75. Arderne's "Hoc est speculum phlebotomie" is discussed in D'Arcy Power, "The Lesser Writings of John Arderne," *Seventeenth International Congress of Medicine*, Sec 23, History of Medicine (London, 1914) pp 108–9. The fifteenth-century Middle English version of his text, "Mirror of Bloodletting," I consulted is Cambridge, Emmanuel College MS. 69, ff 2r–3r.

76. In Chapter 5 of Bk 15, Distinction 2, "De qua latere facienda est flebotomia," of the *Breviarium Bartholomei*, Mirfeld briefly discusses antispasis vs metacentesis as regards a plethoric state, and in Chapter 7. "Quod sit faciendum & quam tempore flebotomia," he discusses the four factors of age, custom, time, and strength in much the same sequence and detail as do the similar passages in the Arderne phlebotomy and the Gonville and Caius MS. 176/97 text. Only comparatively brief

portions of the long compendium have been edited by Hartley and Aldridge, op cit, n 33; and that edition does not include Book 15. I have used British Library Harley MS. 3, ff 292vb–95vb, a late-fourteenth-century codex. Other instances of portions of the text occurring elsewhere may be the case of two brief entries in the "Salernitan Questions" that seem to be akin to the treatise in question (Brian Lawn, *The Prose Salernitan Questions*, Auctores Britannici Medii Aevi 5 [London, 1979]), B 132 and B 243, and a much-altered version of the text in Johannes de Ketham, *Fasciculus medicinae* (Venice, 1491; facsimile reprint with intro by Karl Sudhoff, trans and adapted by Charles Singer [Mailand: Lier, 1924]) f [3v].

77. See above, note 33.
78. Malcolm B. Parkes, "The Influence of the Concepts of *Ordinatio* and *Compilatio* on the Development of the Book," *Medieval Learning and Literature: Essays Presented to R.W. Hunt*, ed J.J.G. Alexander and M.T. Gibson (Oxford: Clarendon, 1976), pp 115–41, and Alastair Minnis, "Late-Medieval Discussions of *Compilatio* and the Role of the *Compilator*," *Beiträge zur Geschichte der deutschen Sprache und Literatur*, *101* (1979), 385–421.
79. James F. Ballard, *A Catalogue of the Medieval and Renaissance Manuscripts and Incunabula in the Boston Medical Library* (Boston: privately printed, 1944), p 15.
80. Letter, 28 September 1981. Marta Powell Harley has undertaken an edition of these texts.
81. Ed Ogden, op cit, note 21.
82. "MS. Rawlinson A. 393: Another Findern Manuscript," *Transactions of the Cambridge Bibliographical Society*, 7 (1980), 447, n. 4. For an example of the clarification made possible by other manuscript readings, see Keiser's " 'Epwort': A Ghost Word in the *Middle English Dictionary*," *English Language Notes*, 15 (1978), 163–4. Keiser promises a forthcoming study of the *Liber* manuscripts.
83. See "Preface," pp viii–x of *The Cyrurgie of Guy de Chauliac*, op cit, note 46.
84. For medical writings of the early Middle Ages, an invaluable catalogue is Augusto Beccaria, *I Codici di Medicina del Periodo Presalernitano* (Rome: Edizioni di Storia e Letteratura, 1956), and for French manuscripts, Ernest Wickersheimer, *Les Manuscrits latins de médecine du haut moyen âge dans les Bibliothèques de France* (Paris: Editions du Centre national de la recherche scientifique, 1966).

ACKNOWLEDGEMENTS

Plates 1 and 2 were reproduced by permission of the owner, Rare Book Room, Elmer Ellis Library, University of Missouri-Columbia.
Plate 3 was reproduced by permission of the Master and Fellows of Gonville and Caius College, Cambridge.

Editing Texts in the History of Early Technology
Bert S. Hall

It is a curious fact that otherwise well-read and astute thinkers often mistake the nature of technology, particularly when technology is considered as a piece of history. It is thus a necessary propaedeutic to begin with some rather elementary observations. First, technology is not science; it differs from science in the twentieth century, and it most emphatically differs from science in the period we are concerned with in this paper, the later Middle Ages and the Renaissance. If science can be loosely defined as the effort to understand nature, and if technology can, equally loosely, be defined as the attempt to manipulate nature for human purposes, then it follows that there is no necessary connection between them. It is true that in our own day, technology is largely based upon knowledge of nature gained through science, but in fact that relationship is barely more than a century old. Earlier science had only the most tangential relationship to technology, either as the source of technical knowledge or in the social realm. Secondly, we must try also to discard all of the categories and subdivisions of technology derived from modern academic and business practices. Just as Medieval and Renaissance technology is not science, so too it is not engineering in anything like the modern sense. Technology was as yet too undifferentiated in the Renaissance to permit modern distinctions. Later I shall try to set forth briefly a list of textual types, but for the moment let me just call attention to a rather gangly corpus of texts from the fourteenth, fifteenth and sixteenth centuries dealing with various arts and crafts; some were clearly handbooks, others treatises, some were notebooks kept privately, while others circulated in narrower or wider circles. Finally, we must accept that in technology there is a gap between the text and the object or process that the text purports to represent. This gap between text and reality is deep in regard to technology, and it requires genuine intellectual effort to understand why.

Derek deSolla Price[1] has remarked on the circumstance that the business of men and women concerned most closely with technology is not to leave textual remains for posterity. Their business was to produce objects and artifacts, not texts. Such people are in that respect utterly unlike those most editors treat. We scholars are people of the book; we study persons who produced texts, whether of poetry or philosophy, novels or mathematical papers. Thus we easily fall into the error of behaving as if we believed all men wish to produce texts. Scholars subordinate objects to texts. In the study of past scientists for example, we may have some access to nontextual remains, specimens, for example or laboratory apparatus, but for the scientists who used them, these objects were but the means to make texts, and so we treat the artifacts as matters for footnotes or appendices. Yet if we wish to take seriously the worlds defined by technology, or the lives of men and women who used technology, if we wish to examine the documents we do have at hand from the realm of technology, then we must begin by accepting a slightly humiliating degradation of our favourite objects of study, texts, to a peripheral status. This is a world in which most men (and women) produce not texts, but artifacts.

The making of texts was not uppermost in the minds of the millions who have used technology, and it is apparent that their work would not have benefited in any substantial way from efforts to translate their experiences into texts. Persons concerned with technology seldom resorted to written documents because such documents were by their very nature irrelevant to the work to be done. I do not mean by this observation merely that technology was the concern largely of illiterate men and women in the period under discussion, though that was surely frequently the case. Nor do I mean that craftsmen were not inclined to risk their livelihoods by committing to writing the "secrets of their trades," though here again that was certainly the case in some instances. On a deeper level I am asserting that those realms of experience and knowledge which we call technology are far too complex to be reduced to mere words and numbers marching across the page.[2] Practice in the pre-modern period was a very special universe of discourse, and we can only rarely catch glimpses into it. About 1122 a German Benedictine named Theophilus Prebyter produced a treatise on the decorative arts called *De diversis artibus* which transcends the limits I am trying here to establish.[3] This remarkable treatise takes us into the world of the monastic workshops where inks are prepared, where gold leaf is made, where bells and chalices are cast. It is a world in which the craftsman had to undergo years of apprenticeship before his judgement was sufficient to allow him to work with materials. When is bronze ready to be cast? Modern practice would answer in terms of the liquid alloy's temperature. Theophilus says when straw cast on top of the molten metal burns with a bright green flame. How quickly should one pour it into the mould? Modern practice answers in terms of viscosity; Theophilus replies that one pours quickly, but stopping often to listen at the sprue for the sound like the crackling of thunder. The colours of things, their smell or taste, how dense something is, how sticky or slick a fluid feels, how plastic or resilient a solid — these are the vital data to a pre-modern craftsman. One had to know how to solder or weld, how to mix mortar and lay it, how to file, or to grind, or to compound mixtures, for these were the skills of the workshop. We, products of an industrial world founded on modern technology, easily lose sight of the degree to which our technological order rationalizes all those matters which Theophilus had to judge by practice. Modern science has affected technical practice through an immense effort that we have expended to rationalize all processes of production. We have invented the means to reduce experience to the level of quantitative data, to substitute for the eye of a craftsman the reading of an instrument, for his judgement the standardized label on a chemical bottle, or for his hand the repetitive action of a machine.

We must recognize that in a world without instruments, standardized labels, or automatic machinery, the essential qualities of the workshop are exactly those which it is most difficult to express in writing. Apprenticeship was an institution made necessary by the very nature of teaching and learning in the world of the workshop. One had to be taught within the rich context of the crafts, face-to-face with one's master, with the tools and materials at hand ready to be held, smelled, or tasted. Craftsmen, whether they had a formal guild structure or not, were living repositories of the knowledge their crafts required. Steeped in the local traditions of their work, these living men were the only effective means by which information about these matters could be transmitted across time and space. Written words could never convey to those without any exposure to the crafts what needed to be taught. Again in the modern world, we are inheritors of a language that has been finely tuned to accommodate the requirements of our sciences and techniques; we have taught generations of students in our polytechnic schools to use certain words in precisely defined ways; we have international commissions whose sole task it is to coin neologisms and to assure their accepted usage in unambiguously defined ways; we teach the same formulae and the same conventions of visual representation to generations of students. A technical paper on almost any subject can be read today by someone half a world away from its author and no shade of meaning need be lost. This semantic uniformity is something we have striven to achieve for the past century and a quarter. Strip away all this, reduce technical matters to the status of ordinary language and ordinary drawings and the result would be, not merely a world without jet aircraft or pocket calculators, but also a world like that of the Middle Ages in which persons with similar technical interests could communicate only within the context of their workshop environments.

These constraints make it clear that the historian interested in early technology cannot expect to find a large number of explicit technical treatises to guide his investigations. It is a truism that we know much more about the history of such machines as windmills and water-wheels from their appearance in documents as diverse as wills or records of litigation than we can obtain from any systematic medieval work on their design, construction, or repair.[4] Indeed, as a general rule, the greater the numbers of craftsmen practicing a given trade, and the more highly organized the craft, the less likely we are to have very much technical literature. We should probably accept as a general maxim that any text which has come down to us from this realm is the product of special circumstances. To take a negative example, we do not have a single document from the entire period of Gothic architecture's dominance in northern Europe that explains in detail what rules were followed by master masons in the design and construction of cathedrals. Masons formed, so far as we can tell, a cohesive craft group (not a guild, for guilds properly speaking are a phenomenon of the sixteenth century) whose members had little need for written documents in their work.[5] Conversely, in fields which engaged the interest of the learned, we can discern a certain over-emphasis on mathematical instruments, chiefly elaborate and sophisticated astronomical instruments and astronomical clocks. Both the underlying mathematical-geometrical basis for such devices and their astronomical-astrological purposes lay firmly within the seven liberal arts. For the most part, works of the mathematical sort are uncompromising in their approaches to their subjects; they give the reader little help with elementary or general matters, concentrating instead on the quantitative information necessary for someone already familiar with the field to design, construct or repair the instrument under discussion. This is understandable if we assume that these works were meant to circulate only within a community of men who had already gained sufficient knowledge to understand the general features and purposes of clocks, astrolabes, or equatoria.[6]

Closely resembling the mathematical instrument treatises are those ancient writings which deal with catapult construction, the design of automata, and the building of pneumatic devices. Oddly enough to the modern mind, the Alexandrian writers seem to have considered designing *ballistae* as a mathematical art, a trait which seems less singular once one becomes aware that catapults had to be proportioned rather strictly according to the size of their main "springs" of twisted rope.[7] Catapult treatises do not produce medieval imitators, but the automata and pneumata literature did, particularly in Islam.[8] In all cases, there is the same impression of uncompromising approach that the mathematical instrument literature conveyed; clearly this is no field for amateurs! The automata and pneumatica have presented modern commentators with considerable difficulties. Their technical contents are usually explicable enough, despite the fact that they were not conceived with inexpert readers in mind, but we have some reservations about expending vast amounts of mechanical ingenuity on what are in fact "toys" for the amusement of adults. More recent scholarship has suggested that the working model figures and trick vessels may have also served important political purposes by impressing both subject and foreign peoples with the skill and artifice at the ruler's command. Likewise, skilled men may have accepted the patronage that their automata brought them as a means of working on interesting technical problems. The fact that a treatise literature in this field exists at all is most likely a reflection of its status at court.[9]

Recipe texts and works giving procedures for the decorative arts form another related category of treatises. These concern themselves principally with chemical transformations and metallurgical recipes appropriate to fields such as painting, gilding, the making of inks, and the working of gold, silver, or copper alloys. The internal technical content of the recipe literature varies according to the circumstances of textual transmission. In the Middle Ages, the decorative arts were originally of interest to monastic foundations where literacy was, of course, the rule. Treatises such as Theophilus' cited above are relatively uncorrupted. Earlier works — the *Mappae clavicula* stand out — were perhaps the victims of well-intentioned but technically unsophisticated monks, for the *Mappae*'s recipes are frequently garbled beyond the ability of modern scholars to reconstruct their meaning.[10] The intended audience of the early recipe texts is almost certainly the technical specialists employed in scriptoria and in monastic workshops to create the decorated objects which the treatises describe. Later examples of the same genre focus on the problem of gunpowder and other pyrotechnic weapons. Beginning in the late thirteenth century (the exact date is still uncertain) with the *Liber ignium* of "Marcus Graecus,"[11] this new form of recipe text reached its most widespread state before the advent of printed texts with the anonymous *Feuerwerkbuch*[12] of the fifteenth century. Gunners might seem an unlikely social group to have a technical literature, but in the absence of a well-defined craft group, mercenary artillerymen were low-level members of courtly circles from at least the mid-fourteenth century. The desire to imitate the higher reaches of courtly society, as well as the complexity of some early pyrotechnic recipes, probably accounts for the gunners' resorting to books.

It certainly makes sense that a technical literature should be directed primarily at those who could be expected to make some use of its technical contents, yet there is another whole strain of technical writing which is distinguished by its authors' apparent intent to direct their efforts at a wider audience. Even in classical antiquity some treatises mixed a highly technical body of information with comments seemingly directed at non-technical readers. Vitruvius' *De architectura* seems to be of this strain, especially in those chapters where Vitruvius exerts himself to establish architects on a somewhat higher social plane than we believe they actually occupied in Augustan Rome. Frontinus' great opus on the water system of ancient Rome is clearly meant to celebrate a splendid engineering accomplishment just as it reveals in great detail the workings of this marvel of hydraulics. Similarly, Vegetius' *Epitoma rei militaris* is both a detailed description of (idealized) military practices, including significant amounts of technical information, and at the same time an advocate's plea for military reform; surely it was meant for eyes other than just the professional officers and tacticians it ostensibly addresses. Possibly the boldest example of the category I am trying to delineate is a work not notably distinguished by its literary merits but which even more than Vegetius sought reforms to save the military might of a dying empire. The anonymous fourth-century treatise *De rebus bellicis* has, despite a revival of interest in it during the Renaissance, never really attained the status of a "classic."[13] Its special pleading in favour of substituting machinery for manpower renders it a slightly risible forerunner of all treatises by inventors who believe their devices can save the world. Nevertheless, as a patent attempt to influence imperial policy, no single piece of writing better confirms the observation that technical treatises can be directed at a non-technical readership.

What sets works of this sort off from their more specialized counterparts, in my opinion, is precisely the fact that they do not assume a prior knowledge of their subjects by their readers. To be sure, the amount of technical information contained in the pages of Vitruvius, Frontinus, or Vegetius may seem daunting to the uninitiated, but by contrast with the truly specialized treatises, the "classic" authors are fairly easy sailing; indeed, that is one reason why we regard them as classics. As a rather striking way of exemplifying this claim we should note that these works sometimes leave modern commentators baffled because they, in an effort to remain suitably superficial, cast their subjects into unclear or incomplete forms, whereas the more technical treatises tend toward the opposite pole of editorial difficulty by failing to make clear the general in their eagerness to concentrate on the specific. We need a generic term for treatises whose readership extended beyond the community of technically competent men. I suggest we call them "courtly" treatises in view of their general purpose of attempting to influence powerful figures in courtly circles. In the form of tractates on military arts (though usually without much technological information), "courtly" treatises appear in medieval Europe, Byzantium, and Islam. A military literature with deeper concentration on technology appears for the first time at the French royal court in the fourteenth century and will be discussed in more detail below. By the fifteenth century works of this sort had developed into the wide-ranging, often illustrated, technological documents we usually associate with Renaissance artist-engineers. The latter group is best known through Leonardo da Vinci's *Notebooks*, but in fact there was a large number of illustrated treatises, note-books and portfolios which circulated in the courts of fifteenth-century Italy and Germany. The examples best known today stem from central Italy, e.g., the *Trattati* of Francesco di Giorgio Martini of Siena,[14] some of which Leonardo is known to have read and copied. Francesco was preceded by another Sienese, Mariano di Jacopo, called "il Taccola," the author of two works on military and civil engineering.[15] Across the Alps an extensive Germanic technical literature was unfolding at about the same time, perhaps inspired by the most widely-cir-culated illustrated compendium, Conrad Kyeser's *Bellifortis*[16] (again, to be discussed in more detail below). Despite the fact that modern editions have tended to emphasize the Italian material, there appears to be an equal volume of technical texts in fifteenth century Germany, e.g., the little tractate mistakenly identified as being from the pen of an "Engineer of the Hussite Wars."[17] Lengthy exposure to these works, both edited and unedited texts, has convinced me that they can be labeled with a term designed to direct our attention toward one of their salient, but overlooked features. I propose to call them "courtly fantasies." .

The term is not meant pejoratively. From the late Middle Ages until the end of the seventeenth century noble and royal courts were centers, not only for artistic and literary activity, but also for technological creativity on a scale that could not easily be duplicated through any other institution. Technically minded men attached to courts must have felt the need to record their designs and schemes, and perhaps even to impress upon the sophisticated world of the court some of the possibilities inherent in the various arts. The large number of such works is the result of their being directed not at the closed universe of practicing technicians, but at the somewhat more fluid world of courtiers and men of affairs. Where circumstances permit us to examine the context in which extant texts of the sort I am discussing were composed, they invariably are related to royal, noble, or municipal courts. Many of them were composed by technological amateurs, in the fourteenth and early fifteenth centuries by physicians preponderantly, and in the later fifteenth century by military architect/engineers/gunners, men who at that time played the role of general technical experts at many courts.

"Fantasy" in my labelling is meant to convey the most difficult feature such works display to an editor (though not necessarily the dominant feature), their fondness for impressive ideas or plans or for bizarre machines or impossible devices. Again, it is in no sense a pejorative term; indeed, I regard the fantastic elements of such texts as among their charming features. Likewise, fantasy is not meant as a *port-manteau* term for elements of life that men of that time took perfectly seriously, e.g., astrology or magic. Rather I mean to suggest that these are works which operate on a plane beyond our grim modern economic deterministic notions of what technology is all about. Courtly fantasies are, if you insist, "coffee table books" of technology for the privileged and wealthy to contemplate and enjoy as an aesthetic experience.[18]

Perhaps these matters will come into clearer focus if I deal with a specific example. The earliest exemplar of the courtly fantasy was composed at the court of King Philip VI of France by the physician to Philip's Queen, Jeanne of Burgundy. Guido da Vigevano, from Pavia, is known to historians of medieval medicine as the author of a little treatise on anatomy based on dissections he had performed himself. In 1335, swept up in the fervor for a renewal of the crusade which Philip and the pope were together promoting, Guido composed a tract titled *Texaurus regis franciae acquisicionis terre sancte de ultra mare*.[19] In it he combined advice on the maintenance of health while on campaign with discussions of the latest in military siegecraft. This combination, so curious to the modern mind, should cause no great concern; Guido's purpose was plainly to contribute to the mood of the event, not to its execution. Quite obviously he chose to present his monarch with intrepid discussion of two topics he happened to know well. Besides, the crusade in question never took place.

Guido's leading idea concerns the shortage of timber in the Holy Land, a serious disability for a medieval army accustomed to foraging its way about and assembling its major siege engines from local supplies of timber. He has in mind to fabricate a series of portable structural elements, mainly poles and planking, from which one could construct siege engines, portable bridges, field defences, and other necessary devices as required. Once such machines had served their purpose, they would be dismantled and transported by horseback to the site of the next siege. To ensure the durability and interchangeability of these elemental parts, Guido proposes that they be reinforced with iron banding at stress points, and in some cases equipped with forged iron slip-keys at critical joints. Guido develops these fundamental ideas in a set of seven chapters taking the reader through the details of constructing various types of shields of towers, ramps and scaling ladders. (Figs 1 and 2) In fact, his text represents the earliest discussion we have of interchangeable parts and the structural use of iron; both were ideas of immense significance at a later period. Their modest pre-history extends from Guido's day to the Industrial Revolution.

Guido then launches into a more elaborate and fantastic set of proposals. He describes pontoon bridges made in small sections; these can be collapsed into compact bundles for transport by horseback. (Fig 3) He describes inflatable flotation collars made of leather in one size proper for horses (Fig 4) and another for men (Fig 5) with which troops may ford rivers

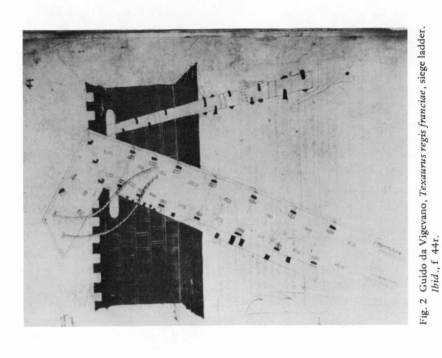

Fig. 2 Guido da Vigevano, *Texaurus regis franciae*, siege ladder. *Ibid.*, f 44r.

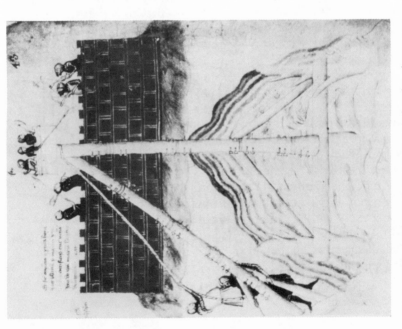

Fig. 1 Guido da Vigevano, *Texaurus regis franciae*, siege tower. Paris, Bibl. Nat., MS. lat. 11015, f 43r.

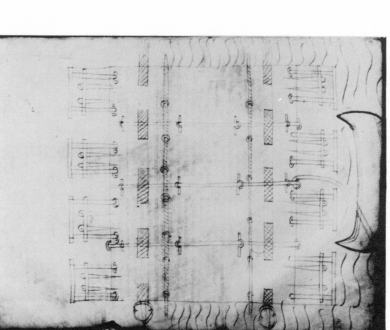

Fig. 3 Guido da Vigevano, *Texaurus regis franciae*, pontoon bridge.
Yale University, Center for British Art, f 10v.

Fig. 4 Guido da Vigevano, flotation device for horse and rider.
Ibid., f 11v.

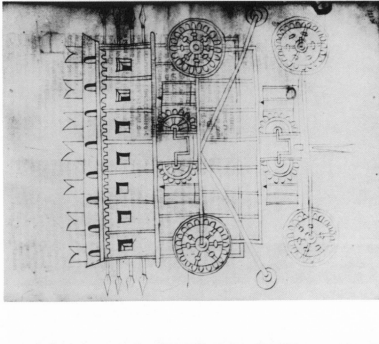

Fig. 6 Guido da Vigevano, war wagon operated by internal cranks and gearing.
Ibid., f 13r.

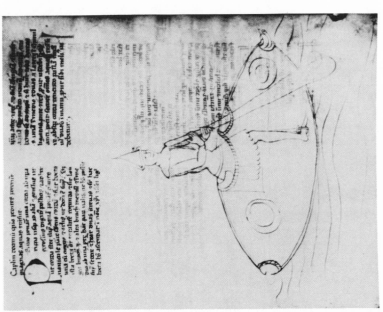

Fig. 5 Guido da Vigevano, flotation for an infantryman.
Ibid., f 12r.

too deep to be crossed. While the practicality of this notion seems dubious, it was nevertheless enthusiastically repeated in treatise after treatise and apparently tried in actual tests from time to time. Reaching deeper into the kingdom of his imagination, Guido describes a covered fighting wagon, a "tank" propelled by men working internal crankshafts and gears; he even includes a steering mechanism operable from within the wagon. (Fig 6) Another chapter concerns a more advanced automobile version of the same machine, this time with a windmill mounted atop it to provide motive force. (Fig 7) Again, while this may seem silly at first glance, Guido's comments and drawings provide us with our first detailed view of the interior of a windmill, a machine which was already 150 years old by his day.

We would be greatly in error to attempt to explain away those features of Guido's tractate that we find unfamiliar by accusing him of technical incompetence. There can be no doubt after a close reading of his words that Guido was a man who knew quite well what he chose to discuss; his vocabulary, his mastery of detail, even his willingness to leave certain matters in the hands of the man in the field — *Ut melius videbitur operanti* — all point to someone who was familiar with machines and their problems in actual use. Neither, I feel, should we think that he is involved in some elaborate joke. Courtly life has its petty byplay and moments of wit, but within the framework of courtly formality, Guido is quite serious about his proposals. We can only understand his text if we adjust our own thinking so as to accord to technological texts the same sort of autonomy that we routinely grant texts in other areas. Guido's business was not to report on what could be done; he saw himself as one to suggest what had never been tried before. His work is not a reflection of reality, but rather a precipitate derived from the technical possibilities of his day as they reacted with his own imagination. The fact that no one could build some of the machines Guido described was no handicap; to later generations it was their exotic character that made them worth copying. It is noteworthy that even after men stopped copying Guido's works

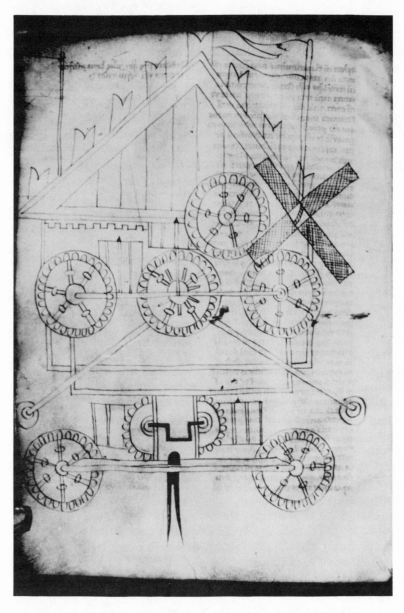

Fig. 7 Guido da Vigevano, war wagon powered by a windmill.
Ibid., f 14v.

as a whole, Roberto Valturio plagiarized some drawings for his *De re militari*, an immensely popular work dating from the 1450's.[20] What Valturio and others copied, and still others repeated, were not Guido's sober realistic proposals, but his more fantastic chapters, particularly the automotive wagons in their two forms. With Guido the locus of imagination moved from the device, which the text could describe, to the text itself, which could then descirbe devices that had never existed.

Shortly before he died in 1405, another physician, Conrad Kyeser aus Eichstätt put the finishing touches on his treatise on military machines and other devices. His title, *Bellifortis*, "Strong in War," only reveals a part of what his work contains: astrology, magical incantations, hydraulic machinery, bathhouses, siege engines, rockets, cannon, multiple-firing guns, crossbows, torture devices, and a chastity belt. This is a vast *summa* of applied and fantastic knowledge, written in exile by a bitter, defeated and dying man. Kyeser, like Guido before him, conceived of his audience as consisting of men at court. Much of his text is framed in dreadful rhyming Latin hexameter. He includes lengthy prefaces and appendices in praise of all the arts and sciences. *Bellifortis* was illustrated by exiled artists departing from the Prague scriptorium and is by any standards a splendid and sumptuous work. It became the most influential technical manuscript of its century. Within two generations, more than twenty copies of *Bellifortis* had been made, and throughout the fifteenth century literally countless adaptations of the work, or partial copies, or outright plagiarizations of parts of it, had spread from Istanbul to London. Some of the illustrations, in fact were adapted to grace printed editions of Vegetius, the ancient Roman writer on strategy, and in this form they continued to be reproduced until deep into the seventeenth century.[21]

To the modern eye, *Bellifortis* appears as a curious mixture of the factual, the mistaken, and the completely fanciful. Kyeser's mixture of technology, magic and his own special blend of the grotesque is a fascinating and sometimes horrifying combination today. For the fifteenth century, however, it was a deeply inspiring source of interest and speculation, Those portions of Kyeser's text which were most frequently copied and mingled with other works are not, in fact, his magic, nor his astrology but rather the more fanciful and imaginative machines amongst his specimens. Like Guido before him, the locus of Kyeser's imagination is the page, not the device; it was for this characteristic above all that his age treasured Conrad's effort.

The resonances which *Bellifortis* found in the German speaking world are difficult to characterize briefly, in part because of the way in which technological information circulated in the courtly tradition. As a rule, an editor who wishes to indicate something about the significance of his text cites the number of manuscript copies of it still extant, as I did above. Yet these courtly manuscripts are different from texts in other fields in that they are highly divisible. What we might call the "atom of information" or the "basic unit of meaning," the smallest portion of a text that can be copied without losing all sense, is , I would estimate, on the order of a chapter's worth of material for most subjects. What is striking about these technical works is that the comparable unit within them is less than one page in length: a recipe, a single drawing, a briefly-noted process. The fifteenth century of course lacked modern notions of copyright; in regard to these texts it put aside its own usual sense of textual integrity as well. Drawings and text, divided into large numbers of discrete units, circulated in an ever-changine kaleidoscope of patterns, grouped and regrouped, shaped and reshaped by each new compositor in turn to meet what he thought his courtly admirers would best appreciate. For the editor, this rather free manner with the text presents an endless series of difficulties; enumerating the "copies" of a text — whatever that word may be taken to mean under these circumstances — is but the least.

The fact that we expect texts to distribute themselves in neat trees should not blind us to deeper levels of meaning apparent in this free pattern of "borrowings." We moderns think of technology as a natural field for priority claims; so did some men of the fifteenth century, yet their promiscuity in

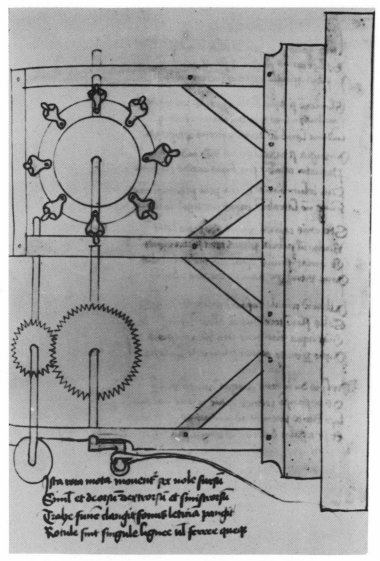

Fig. 8 Conrad Kyeser, *Bellifortis*, bell-ringing machine.
Innsbruck, Ferdinandeum, MS. 16.0.7.

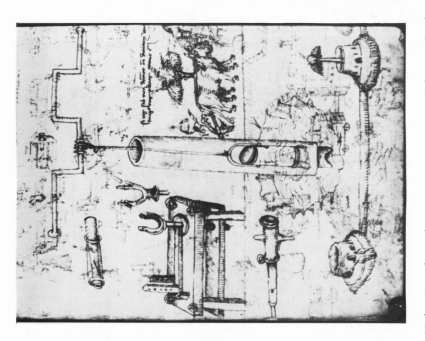

Fig. 9 Mariano Taccola, suction pump operated by crankshaft (note that drawing shows shaft misaligned).

Fig. 10 Anonymous "Hussite," diver in suit with air hose. Munich CLM 197, 1, f 14r.

exchanging ideas, which this manner of circulating texts encouraged, surely militated aginst the idea that technological
ideas were someone's personal property.[22] Instead what we
seem to see is the creation of a field of technical discourse at
least one step removed from the pressing realities of the real
world. The line between the fantastic and the realistic, between
the practical and the frivolous grew blurred. The autonomy
of the text which I mentioned above, its role as the locus of
imagination, was plainly extended beyond any limits known
earlier or generally observed since. The fifteenth-century
authors held reality at a certain distance; they viewed it with
some measure of detachment, considering the possible and
the impossible alike as worthy of exploration on paper.

The results of this new imaginative freedom in technology
are at times rather silly, as in this bell-ringing machine by
Kyeser. (Fig 8) There is no particularly good reason to build
such a machine, and the Latin text in verse holds no clue as
to why one would want to construct it. Nevertheless, each of
its elements was readily available in the repertoire of a technically sophisticated person of the fifteenth century — the
crank, the flywheel, the gears — so why not create the bell-
ringer, on paper if not in the real world? Authors of technical treatises wanted to show what it was possible to achieve.
At other times the results of such wide-ranging imagination
turn up on more practical devices, such as Taccola's depiction
of a suction pump on a crankshaft. (Fig 9) Taccola invented
neither device, but both were relatively new and spreading
quite rapidly in the 1430's when he did this drawing, the
first to depict them in combination. Sometimes one notes
machines or devices that seem to owe much to other realms
of imagination outside the technological, for example a
helmeted diver engaged in salvage work. (Fig 10) He is in some
difficulty owing to the lack of an air pump, but he bears more
than a passing resemblance to the medieval romances about
Alexander the Great, whose adventures also included a deep-
sea dive.[23]

In the hands of a master, of course, this dialogue with the material world's manifold possibilities could result in inventions

utterly without direct precedents. These are always, however, confined to the manuscript page, and I submit that this was both intentional and appropriate in the world of such texts. Leonardo da Vinci, the master of linear perspective sketching, possessed perhaps the greatest capacity of any man living in the fifteenth century to mimic on paper the relationships of objects in three dimensional space. His abilities as an observer who could accurately sketch from nature have frequently been commented upon. I would like to call attention to his other great talent, his ability to envision on the page objects that had never existed at all. In essence, Leonardo's inventive abilities stem from a complex form of "play" with the shapes of objects and with their relationships in space. Figs 11 and 12, for example, show Leonardo speculating through sketches about a problem in clockwork gearing. I shall not go into detail here, but only note that what we can see on this opening of *Madrid Codex I* is a series of designs which I have labelled with the letters A-H. Sketch B represents a piece of an astronomical clock Leonardo saw at Chiaravalle outside Milan, while sketches C through H represent different mechanical means of achieving the same motion. These cannot be merely a catalogue of existing clock parts; other than sketch B none of the devices shown here was built until much later. Indeed, sketch F is mechanically erroneous and cannot work as drawn; sketch H will work, but demands materials that did not exist in Leonardo's day.[24] At another location in the same manuscript (Fig 13), we find Leonardo again speculating on different mechanical possibilities, this time associating superficially different devices such as the ratchet mechanisms in the middle of the scene with the groove cam devices in the upper and lower portions of the page. This ability to associate (and dissociate) on paper led Leonardo through a series of steps too complex to discuss here to a new invention, the regulator pendulum for clockwork. This method of discovery has its limits, of course, for Leonardo never sought to move the pendulum off the page, and thus he missed what Galileo discovered more than a century later, i.e., the inherently superior physical properties of the pendulum-governed clock.[25]

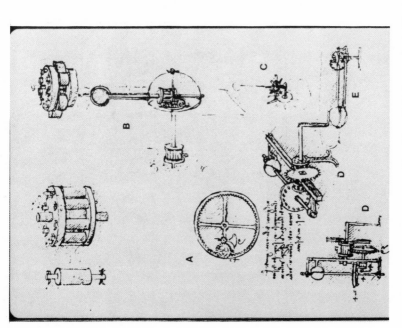

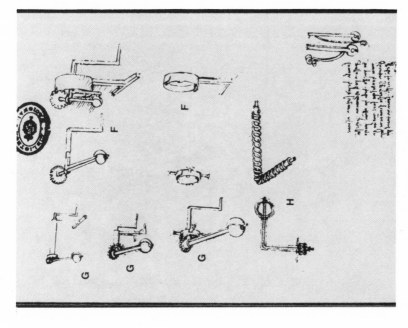

Figs. 11 and 12 Leonardo da Vinci, studies for gearing in lunar dial of Chiaravalle clock showing development of mechanical possibilities. Madrid, Bibl. Nat. MS. 8936, ff 10v–11r.

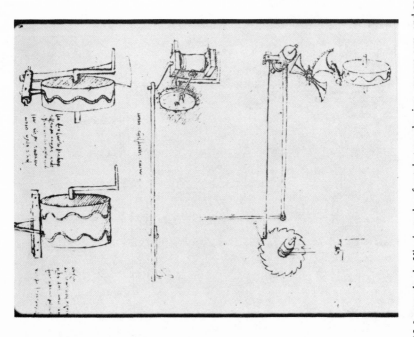

Fig. 13 Leonardo da Vinci, study of ratchet mechanism, groove cam, and oscillating fan escapement.

Fig. 14 Raphael's *Galatea*. Rome, Villa Farnesina.

The example of Leonardo is meant to remind us of the responsibilities we who edit texts like these must undertake. They demand of us a sensitivity to drawings equal to our sensitivity to words and their meanings, for the drawing was in many aspects of technology far more significant than the verbal description or numerical formula. I am distressed to report that the magnificent edition of Leonardo's *Madrid Codices* completed in 1974 by the late Ladislao Reti contains 110 pages of appendices and indices, all devoted to Leonardo's words, none whatsoever to his images. To be fair, image indices are extremely difficult to compile. As the lengthy history of the Princeton Index to Christian Art demonstrates, it requires great dedication and rigid control over one's materials to succeed in making such an index, and computers, those great swift workhorses of modern research, are unfortunately even more blind than they are deaf and mute; it is not yet clear whether we can expect much help from them. Still, in some way we shall have to seek new methods of treating images if we wish to come to terms with men such as Leonardo and the other courtly fantasy authors.

One last sequence of images exemplifies in a deliberately exaggerated fashion another sort of sensitivity I feel editors in this realm should possess. Even if we accept in principle the ideas I have been arguing here concerning technical treatises as bearers of fantasy, it is easy to fall into the error of believing that the only people attentive to those fantasies were technically-minded men. To correct this misconception, I would like to draw upon the work of an art historian, Millard Meiss, concerning an episode from the strange history of the paddle-wheel boat.[26] Fig 14 shows a detail from Raphael's fresco, *Galatea* in the Villa Farnesina in Rome, completed in 1513. Galatea flees from the unwelcome amorous embraces of Polyphemus. Classical figuration of this scene shows Galatea making her escape on the back of a friendly dolphin, but Raphael has equipped his heroine with a more elegant means to escape her fate. Two dolphins pull her as she rides aboard a giant sea-shell, her posture vaguely reminiscent of Botticelli's Venus, but even Venus had to make do without

Fig. 15 Giovanni Fossati's engraving of *Venetia* in a paddle-wheel craft.

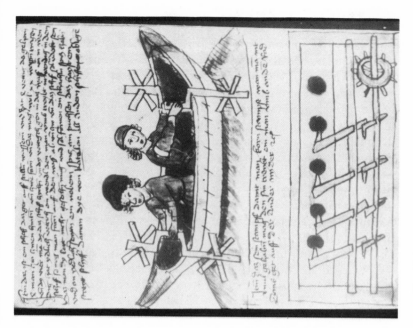

Fig. 17 Anonymous "Hussite," paddle-wheel boat.
Munich, CLM 197, 1, f 17v.

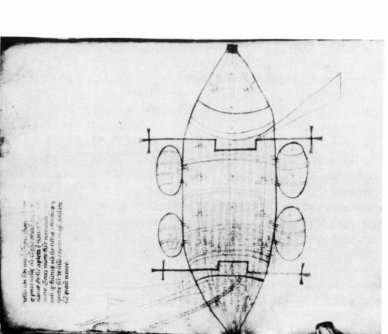

Fig. 16 Guido da Vigevano, paddle-wheel boat (the paddles are represented by the crosses at the ends of the crankshafts).
Yale University, Center for British Art, f 10v.

the latest in marine propulsion devices, the paddle-wheel visible on the starboard side of Galatea's craft. I am unable to hazard an opinion as to how Raphael expected the device to work, since he omitted the power source and its mechanism. Were the paddle-wheel confined to this one example, we might try to shrug it off as a private painterly joke, but in fact Raphael's *Galatea* became quite famous, and its image rather authoritative in such matters. As Meiss masterfully demonstates the scene was publicized by means of Marcantonio Raimondi's engraving based on the fresco and the paddle-wheel became canonical, so to speak, when it appeared in Vincenzo Cartari's iconographic manual for images of the ancient deities in the 17th century. We find paddle-wheel seashells in association with Neptune or Poseidon and his wife Amphitrite in the work of such men as Rubens and Tiepolo (respectively). As late as the middle of the 18th century the image still persisted, as in the engraving (Fig 15) showing a panoramic view of Venice by Giovanni Fossati, done in 1743.

None of the artists who depicted paddle-wheel craft could possibly have seen them in reality, for apart from a few abortive experiments using animals as power, only with the advent of the steam engine did paddle-wheel boats become useful enough to build. Yet even before Raphael, men had envisioned the possibility of such craft, beginning with Guido da Vigevano, who sketched the first European conception of a paddle-wheel boat in 1335 (Fig 16).[27] Thereafter, boats of this sort become almost commonplace within the courtly fantastic technical literature, as exemplified by this German drawing from the early 1470's. (Fig 17) From the courtly texts, paddle-wheel boats spill over into other groups of texts we have not discussed here, chiefly translations from the classics and the printed "Theatres of Machines." On paper, at least, there was a paddle-wheel boat even though none existed elsewhere to be copied. Raphael's successors were responding, I think, not merely to his authority as a painter who could determine iconic forms, but also to the ever-renewed enthusiasm shown in the technical literature for this delightful way of getting over the water. In Meiss's felicitous phrase, "the paddle-wheel

persisted as a valuable fiction, awaiting ... the steam engine."
It seems fitting that an idea which was conceivable, but not
yet capable of full actualization, should have been projected
onto the deities of a mythic past. We have moved rather far afield. Obviously not all that the
technical manuscripts contain takes us so widely beyond the
normal range of editorial concerns as these images. Yet we
who study and edit technological manuscripts from the Middle
Ages and the Renaissance will impoverish ourselves and the
texts we profess to serve if we insist that their only points of
reference be limited to the world of practical, technical, and
detailed realities. Some works were written with one body of
assumptions in mind. Other texts were conceived in a freer
spirit, more distant, less concerned about the demanding realm
of practices. These works need to be edited with an eye that
is sensitive to their internal and their external dialogues, to
the world of possibilities they envision, and to the echoes
their imaginative visions sometimes raised in the larger world.

NOTES

1. "On the Historiographic Revolution in the History of Technology,"
   Technology and Culture, 15 (1974), 42–48, esp 44–45. Price couches
   his remark in terms of Robert Merton's discussion of the differences in
   proprietary rights between science and technology, and he means them
   to illustrate a point made only in passing. I am unaware of any discussion in the literature of the deeper significance of this issue for method-
   ology or historiography.
2. In this matter I am developing an argument first put forth by A.R. Hall
   in regard to science and technology in the 17th and 18th centuries. See his
   "The Scholar and the Craftsman in the Scientific Revolution," in Marshall
   Clagett (ed), *Critical Problems in the History of Science* (Madison, Wisc.,
   1969), pp 3–32 and also "What Did the Industrial Revolution in Britain
   Owe to Science?" in Neil McKendrick (ed), *Historical Perspectives:
   Studies in English Thought and Society in Honour of J.H. Plumb*
   (London, 1974), pp 129–151.
3. Ed and Trans C.R. Dodwell (London, 1961). Cf the annotated trans-

lation by J.G. Hawthorne and C.S. Smith (Chicago, 1963). The examples employed above all derive from Book 3, chapter 85, *De campanis fundendis*.

4. B.B. Blaine, "The Enigmatic Water-Mill," in B.S. Hall and D.C. West (eds), *On Pre-Modern Technology and Science: Studies in Honor of Lynn White, jr.* (Los Angeles, 1976), pp 163–76.

5. Curiously, the earliest written instruction manuals on Gothic construction stem from the late fifteenth century, when the style was going into decline. See Lon R. Shelby, *Gothic Design Techniques: The Fifteenth-Century Design Booklets of Mathes Roriczer and Hanns Schmuttermayer* (Carbondale, Ill., 1977).

6. For a sample of the texts dealing with only one instrument from one national library, see Emmanuel Poulle, "L'astrolabe médiéval d'après les manuscrits de la Bibliothèque Nationale," *Bibliothèque de l'Ecole des Chartes, 112* (1954), 81–103. The distinction between mathematical instrument treatises and other types of technological writing is developed further in my "Giovanni de 'Dondi and Guido da Vigevano: Notes Toward a Typology of Medieval Technological Writings," *Annals of the New York Academy of Sciences, 314* (1978), 126–42.

7. The standard discussion of the Alexandrian writers is A. G. Drachmann, *Ktesibios, Philon, Heron* (Copenhagen, 1948) and more recently *The Mechanical Technology of Greek and Roman Antiquity* (Madison, Wisc., 1963). See also E.W. Marsden, *Greek and Roman Artillery*, 2 vols (Oxford, 1969–71).

8. Donald R. Hill has produced several recent text editions and studies in this field, including the pneumatic devices by the Banū Musā (Boston/Dordrecht, 1979), the *Book of Knowledge of Ingenious Mechanical Devices* by Ibn al-Razzāz al-Jazarī (Boston/Dordrecht, 1974). See also his "A Treatise on Machines by Ibn Mu 'adh Abu 'Abd Allah al-Jayyāni," *Journal for the History of Arabic Sciences,1* (1977), 33–46.

9. D.J. de Solla Price, "Automata and the Origins of Mechanism and Mechanistic Philosophy," *Technology and Culture, 5* (1964), 9–23 and Silvio Bedini, "The Role of Automata in the History of Technology," *Technology and Culture, 5* (1964), 24–42. For a comment on the political significance of the automata in antiquity, cf Lynn White, jr. "Technological Development in the Transition from Antiquity to the Middle Ages," in *Tecnologia, economia e societa nel mondo romano* (Como, 1981), pp 239–40.

10. C.S. Smith and J.G. Hawthorne, *Mappae Clavicula: A Little Key to the World of Medieval Techniques (Transactions of the American Philosophical Society*, N.S. *64*, pt 4; Philadelphia, 1974).

11. For the *Liber ignium* M. Berthelot's *La chemie au moyen âge* (1893; reprint Amsterdam, 1967), pp 100–20 remains one of the most useful. Cf J.R. Partington, *A History of Greek Fire and Gunpowder* (Cambridge, 1960), pp 42–63. The most complete list of manuscripts was prepared by D. Loth (Unpublished seminar paper, University of Toronto, 1979).

12. W. Hassenstein, *Das Feuerwerkbuch von 1420* (Munich, nd [1941]) should be used with great caution.

13. E.A. Thompson, *A Roman Reformer and Inventor: Being a New Text of the Treatise De rebus bellicis* (Oxford, 1952). On the revival of this work during the Renaissance see B. Gille, *Engineers of the Renaissance* (Cambridge, Mass, 1966), pp 16–18.

14. Corrado Maltese (ed), Francesco di Giorgio Martini, *Trattati di architettura, ingegneria e arte militare* (Milan, 1967).

15. Works by Taccola in modern editions include his *De machinis*, ed G. Scaglia (Wiesbaden, 1971) and his earlier *De ingeneis*, ed G. Scaglia and F. Prager (Cambridge, Mass, 1972).

16. G. Quarg (ed), Conrad Kyeser aus Eichstätt, *Bellifortis*, 2 vols. (Düsseldorf, 1967).

17. Bert S. Hall, *The Technological Illustrations of the So-Called Anonymous of the Hussite Wars: Codex latinus monacensis 197, Part 1* (Wiesbaden, 1979).

18. For further comment on the fifteenth-century texts in general cf Gille (note 13 above) and my *"Der meister sol auch kennen schreiben und lesen:* Writings about Technology ca. 1400–ca. 1600 and Their Cultural Implications," in D. Schmand-Besserat (ed) *Early Technologies: Invited Lectures on the Middle East*, Vol 3 (Los Angeles, 1978), pp 47–58.

19. Guido's text exists in a partial translation (military portion only) by A.R. Hall in B. Hall and D.C. West (note 4 above), pp 11–52. This is based on the best known-manuscript, Paris Bibl. Nat. Ms. lat. 11015. For other manuscripts and Guido's medical works see my "Production et diffusion de certains traités de techniques au moyen âge," in G. Allard (ed) *Les arts mécaniques au moyen âge* (Montréal, 1982), pp 140–67.

20. Roberto Valturio, *De re militari* (*Editio princeps*: Verona, 1472). For a list of earlier manuscripts, see Gille (note 13 above), p 250.

21. B. Hall (note 17 above) provides a full list on pp 121–33.

22. An interesting study is found in Ladislao Reti, "Francesco di Giorgio Martini's Treatise on Engineering and Its Plagiarists," *Technology and Culture, 4* (1963), 287–98.

23. D.J.A. Ross, *Alexander and the Faithless Lady: A Submarine Adventure* (London, 1967) traces the legends of the conquerer's underwater exploits and their effects on the medieval imagination.

24. For fuller explication, see B.S. Hall and I. Bates, "Leonardo, the Chiaravalle Clock and Epicyclic Gearing: A Reply to Antonio Simoni," *Antiquarian Horology, 8* (1976), 910-17.

25. B.S. Hall, "The New Leonardo," *Isis, 67* (1976), 463-76 develops this argument in detail.

26. Millard Meiss, "Raphael's Mechanized Seashell: Notes on a Myth, Technology and Iconographic Tradition," in U.E. McCracken *et al* (eds) *Gatherings in Honor of Dorothy E. Miner* (Baltimore, 1974), pp 317-32.

27. Meiss derives Raphael's image ultimately from a paddle-wheel boat proposed in late antiquity in *De rebus bellicis* (note 13 above). Yet Guido's image antedates the revival of interest in the ancient text, indicating that some other intermediate source needs to be located. Chinese paddle-wheel boats are the most likely candidates; see J. Needham, *Science and Civilisation in China,* Vol 4, pt 2 (Cambridge, 1965), pp 413 *et seq.*

ACKNOWLEDGEMENTS

fig 1,2 Paris Bibl. Nat.; figs 3, 4, 5, 6, 7, & 16, Yale University; fig 8, Innsbrück, Ferdinandeum; fig 9, Bayerische Staatsbibl.; figs 10 & 17, Bayerische Staatsbibl. and Dr Ludwig Reichert Verlag; figs 11 & 12, Madrid, Bibl. Nat. & McGraw-Hill Book Company; fig 14, Rome, Villa Farnesina.

Problèmes d'Edition de la Correspondence d'un homme Prodigieux: Marin Mersenne
Armand Beaulieu

Pour mieux comprendre les problèmes auxquels se trouve assujetti l'éditeur de la Correspondance d'un homme aussi prodigieux que Mersenne, je me crois obligé de vous présenter en quelques mots le personnage.

En 1611, alors que les travaux de la Place Royale étaient presque terminés, l'ordre religieux des Minimes fonde un monastère tout près de cette place tranquille, mais nouveau centre élégant de Paris. La discipline de l'ordre était austère, les moines étaient tenus à une vie très stricte, mais dans leur église se réunissaient, auprès d'Anne d'Autriche, les nobles et les grands commis de l'Etat; leur infirmerie modèle était ouverte à tous, aux plus pauvres comme aux plus riches.[1]

C'est à ce monastère que se présenta en juillet 1611, avant même qu'en soient commencés les grands travaux, le jeune Mersenne, alors âgé de 22 ans. Il devait rester toute sa vie, c'est à dire jusqu'à sa mort en 1648, dans ce monastère, à part quelques courts·voyages et deux ans passés à Nevers. Et pourtant ce moine fut un homme prodigieux. Sa famille était assez modeste et ce n'est pas chez elle qu'il aurait pu être aidé du point de vue intellectuel. Mais il possédait plusieurs qualités qui le prédisposaient à une vie d'étude singulière: il aimait travailler à sa table, aligner des suites de chiffres compliqués, à plaisir, chercher la raison de tous les phénomènes physiques, proposer au public en épais volumes, le résultat de ses réflexions et de celles de son temps qu'il estimait sérieuses et convaincantes. De plus, il complétait ces qualités par le désir de voir par lui-même, qu'il s'agisse d'expériences balistiques ou d'hypothèses sur le vide. Il voulait des interlocuteurs pour corroborer ses propres théories, profiter de leurs interprétations ou proposer un travail nouveau. Ces interlocuteurs, s'il ne les trouvait pas sur place, il allait les chercher, par la correspondance, jusque dans les lointaines provinces ou à l'étranger (Hollande, Italie, Espagne, Angleterre, Suisse, Pologne...). A eux tous, il posait quelques problèmes, les mettait au courant des réponses qu'il avait reçus par ailleurs, réclamait des nouvelles sur la vie scientifique, les personnes, leurs découvertes, leurs productions. Lui-même envoyait à chacun des détails sur les nouvelles parutions de livres, sur ce qu'il voyait autour de lui, sur les idées qui sans arrêt jaillissaient de sa pensée.

Nous ne pouvons nous arrêter aujourd'hui sur les ouvrages de ce savant. Nous nous limiterons à sa correspondance et aux problèmes qui s'y rattachent. Jusqu'ici, 14 volumes in-8º, de 600 à 800 pages chacun ont paru. Deux autres volumes sont prévus, puis se seront les tables ... c'est suffisant pour essayer de tirer les leçons d'un tel travail.

Sur les divers volumes de la *Correspondance*, commencée en 1641, on voit figurer divers noms d'éditeurs qui se sont succédé. Nous fumes chargés de continuer la collection à partir du t. XIII.

Tous ces rédacteurs successifs s'imposèrent de suivre la même méthode pour conserver à l'oeuvre une unité certaine et un intérêt continuel.

Le premier problème dont se sont préoccupés les éditeurs

de la *Correspondance de Mersenne*, c'est la recherche des documents. On ne peut donner de lois générales pour un tel travail, chaque correspondance présentant un cas d'espèce: une recherche passionnante s'ouvre à nous qui nécessite de l'attention avec une profonde honnêteté de travail et qui s'applique tout aussi bien aux imprimés qu'aux manuscrits.

1º — Les imprimés.

a) D'abord le plus facile et pourtant qui demande de nombreuses heures de patience, c'est de se préoccuper des lettres *déjà publiées*, non pas pour économiser son propre travail, mais surtout parce qu'on a la chance d'être guidé de façon assez sûre par les savants qui se sont occupés des documents. C'est ainsi que vouloir éditer des lettres de Gassendi sans avoir lu auparavant le magnifique travail publié à Lyon en 1756 ou le recueil des lettres de Sorbière composé par son fils, serait une marque de suffisance intellectuelle assez suspecte. Pour Mersenne, il n'existe pas, avant notre édition, de publication entièrement consacrée à sa correspondance. Dans un récent article publié dans *Les Nouvelles de la République des Lettres*,[2] nous avons indiqué 34 références où l'on peut retrouver, imprimées, des lettres de Mersenne. Même si parfois plusieurs lettres figurent dans tel ou tel document cité, le nombre total est infime par rapport à ce qui restait à publier.

b) A ce moment de nos recherches, se pose une question qu'il faut résoudre: c'est celle des épîtres-dédicaces qui précèdent certains traités imprimés de Mersenne. Faut-il n'y voir qu'une extension du texte imprimé? La question est discutée et différemment résolue par les éditeurs de diverses correspondances. Depuis le début, les éditeurs de Mersenne les ont données intégralement. C'est le moyen de préciser la pensée de l'auteur, mais aussi de voir auprès de qui il trouvait accueil d'amitié, ambition politique ou secours d'argent. Les personnages auxquels Mersenne dédie ces épîtres-dédicaces peuvent être des personnalités illustres, surtout des grands commis de l'Etat, ou des ecclésiastiques. Un seul cas un peu curieux: il dédie les *Sagittarum, Jaculorum et aliorum Missilium Jactus* à Jean-Jacques de Barillon, Président de la Première Chambre des enquêtes,[3] un homme très droit, mais peu politique, toujours mêlé à des revendications de principe, "accoutumé à la prison" comme dira plus tard Voltaire à son sujet. Faut-il voir dans l'attitude de Mersenne une douce mise en garde? Je ne m'arrête davantage sur cette recherche de textes imprimés, qui est indispensable.

2º — Mais vient ensuite une nouvelle démarche: la recherche des manuscrits dont on n'a pas encore parlé. Cette démarche sera à la fois double et complémentaire: la première concernera les lettres reçues par le personnage qui intéresse l'éditeur; la seconde, celles qu'il a envoyées.

a) On comprend qu'il soit plus facile de commencer par des lettres reçues par un personnage, car il a pu et même il a dû garder par devers lui une documentation qu'il était seul à posséder. Parfois ce genre de notes ont été pieusement gardées par des héritiers, parfois elles ont été mises en sûreté dans des bibliothèques ou des dépôts d'archives. Dans le cas de Mersenne, nous avons été favorisés par le sort: il existe à la Bibliothèque Nationale de Paris trois gros in-folios reliés et marqués aux armes des Minimes.[4] Ce fut le P. Hilarion de Coste qui s'occupa, après le passage de Roberval (qui en avait dérobé quelques unes) de recueillir les lettres conservées par Mersenne et de les réunir en volumes. Il dut faire ce travail assez tôt si l'on en croit une note inscrite au premier folio du nº 6204. En outre, on relève chez Baillet (l'éditeur de Descartes) la mention formelle du "tome Ier des Lettres manuscrites du P. Mersenne." Les 3 volumes risquèrent d'être mis en pièces et vendus par le trop célèbre Italien Libri qui, à la fin du XIXe siècle, s'était approprié plus de 3.000 manuscrits pour établir sa fortune.[5] Ces volumes ne semblent pas avoir souffert pour être passés entre ses mains. Quant au 4ème volume des manuscrits de Mersenne, il avait été égaré plus tôt, car on possède des preuves de sa disparition à une date antérieure.

Outre les lettres adressées à Mersenne dans les trois volumes que nous venons d'indiquer, il existe des documents qui sont classés dans d'autres dossiers ou dans d'autre bibliothèques. C'est ainsi que la plupart des lettres de Descartes sont conservées à la Bibliothèque de l'Institut ou à la Sorbonne. Ces anomalies peuvent s'expliquer par des circonstances fortuites ou par des appartenances à tel ou tel collectionneur qui se serait installé en province ou à l'étranger. C'est le cas par exemple de la Collection Charvey à Lyon ou de la Collection Hohendorf à Vienne en Autriche. Une importante lettre de Torricelli à Mersenne s'est retrouvée par une série d'avatars au Chateau de Mariemont en Belgique.

De ce monde de collectionneurs, il ne faut pas oublier les copistes qui, ne pouvant conserver des originaux, se contentaient de relever des textes qui, actuellement, nous deviennent si précieux. Mersenne lui-même s'est-il servi de copistes lorsqu'il n'avait pas le temps de copier un texte auquel il tenait? Quelques allusions et quelques rares exemples nous permettent de l'assurer, mais il ne semble pas avoir abusé de cette facilité.

b) Malgré certaines difficultés, on le voit, il n'était pas tellement compliqué, avec un peu de patience et de méthode, d'exhumer à Paris, dans quelques villes de province ou même à l'étranger des lettres reçues par Mersenne. Mais la démarche inverse, c'est à dire retrouver des lettres expédiées par Mersenne, présentait une assez lourde tâche: il fallait d'abord se mettre en quête des personnages à qui Mersenne avait écrit ou, à tout au moins, des villes où ils avaient demeuré. Ainsi l'on ait dans ces villes ou chez ces personnages, conservé soigneusement les lettres de Mersenne. Cette quête n'a rien donné pour Ricci, le mathématicien de Rome. Elle fut très fructueuse[6] pour Galilée et Torricelli dont beaucoup de documents ont été recueillis par la Biblioteca nazionale di Firenze, ce qui vient en complément de ce que l'on retrouve à Venise ou à Faenza. Près de 60 lettres de Mersenne ont été conservées dans la Bibliothèque Universitaire de Leyde: elles ont été écrites à André Rivet, ce pasteur protestant, grand ami de Mersenne, qui devait devenir l'un des curateurs de la célèbre Université de Breda.[7] Avec le philosophe Descartes, nous avons eu moins de chance: Mersenne et lui s'écrivaient souvent plusieurs fois par mois[8] et cependant en tout et pour tout, l'on n'a trouvé que 25 lettres: c'est que Descartes, même s'il tenait grand compte des avis de Mersenne (et nous savons qu'il le faisait) n'aimait pas beaucoup garder la correspondance qu'il recevait. A la rigueur, il faisait recopier certains textes, mais il y eut aussi des difficultés de transport avec un naufrage et la précieuse collection de textes qui resta trois jours au fond de l'eau[9] avant de parvenir à l'Institut.... Nous ne pouvons énumérer ici tous les correspondants à qui s'adressait Mersenne, mais signalons encore les deux Huygens qui ont comservé les lettres de Mersenne, actuellement gardées à l'université de Leyde et aux Archives de la Maison d'Orange. Il en est de même pour le musicien Jean-Albert Ban.

Ici encore il faut rechercher les collectionneurs, mais dans l'autre sens. Il faut manier avec patience et persévérance les répertoires et les fiches de manuscrits dans les grandes bibliothèques.... Il faut savoir suivre les catalogues de vente. C'est ainsi par exemple qu'une lettre concernant Mersenne fut successivement mise en vente avec les manuscrits de Filon (1878), de Bovet (1887) et de Fatio (Paris, 1931). Le fac-similé d'un fragment en fut imprimé en 1887 à l'occasion de la vente Bovet. On peut voir ce fac-similé dans les *Opere di Ev. Torricelli*. Mais Mme Tannery obtint une copie de la lettre entière, grâce à l'amabilité de Charavey. Elle a été intégralement publiée dans la *Correspondance de Mersenne*.[10]

3° — Lettres écrite *à* Mersenne ... Lettres écrites *par* Mersenne ... Je pense que vous voyez les difficultés auxquelles on est confronté. Mais il est une troisième série de lettres dont il faut s'occuper: les lettres *au sujet* de Mersenne. En effet des renseignements donnés par de tierces personnes peuvent éclairer les questions, résoudre les problèmes, en donner les prolongements. Il faut donc s'imposer de fournir au lecteur des informations de ce genre. Comment pourrait-on comprendre les recherches de Mersenne sur le vide si l'on passait sous silence les lettres de Desnoyers à Hevelius ou à Roberval,[11] celles de Pascal à Roberval. Comment pourrait-on deviner la méfiance des mathématiciens italiens à l'égard de Mersenne si l'on ne citait pas ce qu'en disaient Torricelli, Ricci ou Cavalieri? Comment pouwrait-on apprécier l'attitude de Mersenne vis à vis des mathématiciens italiens à l'égard de qui sont échangées entre Const. Huygens et Rivet,[12] entre

Pell et Cavendish? Et alors, si la réponse est positive, il faut de nouveau se pencher sur les manuscrits et appliquer les considérations énumérées plus haut, il faut consulter les documents de l'époque. A quel moment s'arrêter? Quelles lettres "d'autres" personnages faut-il choisir? La réponse dépend de la culture des éditeurs et des appréciations dont ils sont les seuls juges. Le plus cruel, c'est qu'il arrive un moment où l'on doit s'arrêter de chercher, alors qu'on voudrait continuer.... Tout ce travail peut sembler fastidieux et pourtant c'est ce qui permet de passer à l'étape suivante, celle de l'établissement du texte.

L'établissement du texte est évidemment essentiel, car c'est de lui que dépendent l'honnêteté et la valeur du travail. A la grande rigueur, tel ou tel document peut avoir été oublié: il suffira de le replacer dans l'un ou l'autre des tomes suivants. Mais un contresens ou un non-sens dans un texte, même si l'on essaie de le reprendre dans des *errata* ultérieurs, dénotent un certain manque de travail ou une incapacité plus ou moins foncière de la part de l'interprète. Voici les points où doit l'on exercer sa sagacité:

1º — Evidemment — et je ne m'arrêterai pas sur ce point — il faut posséder une connaissance préalable des sciences telles qu'elles sont connues au XVIIᵉ siècle: mathématiques, physique surtout, astronomie, chimie et sciences de la terre.... Mais il faut aussi la connaissance de la philosophie, de l'exégèse biblique, de la théologie....

2º — L'établissement du texte suppose une connaissance préalable des écritures, des abréviations, de l'orthographe, de la ponctuation et, en général, de la langue de l'époque. Il est certain qu'on n'écrit pas de la même façon en onciales, en lettres gothiques ou en écriture du XVIIᵉ siècle. Chez Mersenne, la difficulté de l'écriture réside surtout dans les lettres initiales dont plusieurs se ressemblent (par exemple les *c, r, e*) et dans les finales trop souvent terminées ou remplacées par une boucle ou un crochet. Quant aux mots les plus courants (*est, et, par, comme*), ils sont notés par des ligatures assez similaires les unes aux autres. Chez Mersenne l'orthographe, celle du

XVIIe siècle évidemment, est correcte (sauf pour les noms propres). Il n'en va pas de même dans les textes de ses correspondants chez qui règne la plus douce fantaisie. C'est le cas par exemple de quelques minimes, sans doute d'origine assez modeste et qui semblent méconnaître les premiers rudiments du français. Parmi les laics, Pierre Desnoyers secrétaire à Varsovie de la reine Louise-Marie écrit beaucoup, mais semble mépriser toute règle courante. Chez Mersenne, du moins à la différence de certains, le français est correct, vivant et coloré. Chez lui et aussi chez ses correspondants, le latin est excellent, parfois seulement un peu recherché (je pense par exemple à une énumération adressée au début du *Traité de Mécanique* à Claude Marcel, sieur de Bouqueval, et concernant les noms d'instruments *ad honestè commodeque vivendum necessaria*).[13] Le grec est représenté par des mots que l'on trouve plus expressifs que le latin ou le français, rarement par des explications complètes. Quant à l'hébreu, on ne se sert que de l'hébreu biblique pour préciser ou interpréter une citation de l'Ecriture Sainte ou pour discuter de la vocalisation des Massorètes. Cela va même si loin que Mersenne n'hésite pas à proposer à Buxtorf de Bâle des traductions fantaisistes faites par certains de ses amis et qu'excuserait peut-être une notation vocalique différente.[14] Pour les langues modernes et leur orthographe, il faut savoir se plier aux bizarreries de l'époque: il s'agira surtout de l'italien, de l'anglais et du néerlandais.

3° — Quoi qu'il en soit de ces pratiques ou de ces routines, les éditeurs successifs de la *Correspondance de Mersenne* se sont imposé, quand ils ont affaire avec un manuscrit, de suivre scrupuleusement, sauf pour les *u* et les *v*, les graphies employées par l'auteur, même en cas de fautes d'orthographe, d'incorrections, de redites ou de contradictions ou encore en cas d'abus de majuscules. Pourtant quand une correction s'impose à l'occasion d'une abréviation obscure ou d'une omission flagrante ou d'un cas d'espèce évident, ces éditeurs portent la correction dans le texte, mais indiquent la forme originale dans les variantes qui s'inscrivent au bas de la page sous le texte et indépendamment des notes du commentaire.

Depuis le début de la collection, on s'est permis de sou-

ligner dans le texte le titre des ouvrages cités par Mersenne ou
ses correspondants. Cette pratique est très utile pour un
lecteur qui voit ainsi plus rapidement le sujet dont on parle.
Mais, pour ma part, j'avoue que selon la rigueur scientifique,
on pourrait reprocher cette façon de faire puisqu'il s'agit d'une
interprétation d'un texte qui devrait se suffire à lui-même. Il
faut pourtant convenir qu'elle ne trahit pas tellement le texte,
alors que pour un lecteur pressé, c'est une aide non négligeable.

Le seul changement que l'on ait introduit à partir du tome
XIII, c'est celui de garder la distinction entre les u et les v ce
qui permet de se rapprocher plus parfaitement de l'écriture
du XVIIe siècle et n'est pas trop compliqué pour le public
moderne.

4º — Ce qui peut le dérouter au contraire, et pourtant la
démarche est logique, c'est qu'une lettre dont on ne possède
pas le manuscrit, mais que l'on a trouvé dans une édition im-
primée, présentera une orthographe et une typographie souvent plus modernes que d'autres lettres contemporaines. On
en comprend la raison et il serait mal venu d'essayer de retrouver l'orthographe ou la présentation primitives. Il suffira au
lecteur de jeter un coup d'oeil aux références de la lettre pour
savoir où on l'a prise et s'il s'agit d'un original ou d'une copie.

5º — Le cas des figures pose un autre problème.

a) Il est évident que l'on doit les présenter quand elles
ont été imaginées par les rédacteurs des lettres. Mais comment
s'y prendre dans un livre du XXe siècle? Grâce aux procédés
les plus modernes, doit-on utiliser des photocopies pour offrir
aux lecteurs des documents tels que les ont dessinés les auteurs? Les éditeurs de Mersenne ont répondu par la négative
et ont préféré, sauf de rares exceptions, faire dessiner à nouveau les figures et cette pratique semble la meilleure. En effet,
trop souvent les dessins originaux sont un peu approximatifs,
tracés sans l'aide d'une règle ou d'un compas, parfois raturés
souvent de formats différents. Il convenait de leur accorder
tout l'intérêt que primitivement l'on avait voulu leur donner,
en renouvelant leur clarté et en présentant des constructions
nettes et pratiques. On a toujours respecté dans les figures les
lettres employées dans le texte.

b) Chaque volume de la *Correspondance de Mersenne* comprend au moins trois ou quatre planches hors-texte. Ces planches rompent la monotonie des gros volumes, elles contribuent aussi à un renouvellement d'intérêt. Elles sont choisies avec soin, éclairent les textes et se rapportent aux questions évoquées dans le volume. Assez fréquemment, ce sont des portraits de savants, parfois des renseignements sur certains lieux. C'est ainsi qu'on a pu illustrer les recherches du P. Maignan en montrant "l'astrolabe" que Mersenne a pu contempler lors de son voyage à Rome.[15] On a pu reproduire aussi une vue de la maison de campagne des Huygens, endroit d'où Christiaan envoyait à Mersenne ses fameuses lettres.[16] Dans le tome XV sera offerte une représentation du monastère de Chaumont-le-Bourg en Auvergne où Thibaut faisait des expériences pour Mersenne.

Nous pouvons maintenant progresser dans notre étude de la correspondance de Mersenne: après la recherche des documents, après l'établissement du texte, il faut s'occuper de la 3ème partie: le commentaire.

Contrairement à d'autres éditions de correspondances où l'on s'abstient de tout commentaire, l'avantage de la *Correspondance de Mersenne*, c'est que, dès le début, les éditeurs ont voulu en éclairer le texte par des explications qui guideraient les lecteurs. Nous allons essayer de caractériser ces explications.

1° — La première explication que l'on attend est celle de la *localisation* et la *connaissance des documents*. D'où provient le manuscrit? de quelle ville? de quelle bibliothèque? avec quelles références? est-ce une copie ou un texte original? est-il signé? S'il s'agit d'une copie, peut-on faire confiance au copiste? ce copiste est-il connu par ailleurs? Le lieu où l'on a trouvé le document permet-il des recoupements avec d'autres pièces? A-t-on trouvé des copies différentes en d'autres lieux? Quel texte a-t-on choisi de reproduire? pourquoi? Donnera-t-on les variantes de certaines copies? Cette question demande d'être posée, mais la réponse n'est pas forcément affirmative puisque les copies en question peuvent être semblables ou que l'une ou l'autre ne présente aucune valeur. Il faut indiquer aussi si la lettre a été publiée. A quelle époque? par qui? entièrement ou en partie? dans quel but? S'il en existe encore un manuscrit, la première publication est-elle correcte? Si le manuscrit a disparu, peut-on faire confiance à cette première publication?

2º — La deuxième explication que l'on attend, c'est celle de la *chronologie*. Il importe en effet de présenter aux utilisateurs des textes qui se suivent dans le temps et peuvent ainsi éclairer d'autres textes.

a) Quand une lettre est datée et signée, il n'y a pas de difficulté à classer avant ou après une autre. Mais quand elle ne porte pas de date, les éditeurs doivent chercher une certitude par l'étude du texte, par des allusions à des lettres précédentes ou à des faits contemporains, par des références bibliographiques. En cas de doute, une approximation à la rigueur est possible et l'on date la lettre "aux environs de juillet" ... ou bien "avant le 1er octobre" ... ou bien "après le 3 décembre" ... Dans des cas plus compliqués, on devra se contenter d'indiquer l'année. Et si cette dernière approximation est impossible, on en sera réduit à tout réunir dans un supplément au dernier volume. Cette question de chronologie est surtout très importante en Histoire des Sciences, alors qu'il est indispensable de marquer et de sérier l'évolution des idées, des doctrines et des découvertes.

b) Très voisine de la chronologie est la recherche qui consiste à préciser l'enchainement des correspondances : cette lettre est-elle une réponse à une lettre précédente? de quelle époque? dans quelle optique se situe-t-elle? est-elle au contraire une demande de renseignements? quand recevra-t-elle une réponse? L'auteur fait-il exprès d'omettre certaines questions? pourquoi?

A partir de la troisième explication que les lecteurs sont en droit d'attendre, les éditeurs débordent du texte proprement dit pour l'éclairer par des renseignements qu'ils vont chercher à l'extérieur d'une lettre. Cette troisième explication concerne l'identification des personnages.

3º — L'identification des *personnages cités* est indispensable et, avec Mersenne ou ses correspondants, cette démarche s'impose si l'on veut comprendre leurs préoccupations et leurs intérêts. Par exemple, il est intéressant d'identifier les jeunes Sociniens qui sont venus voir Mersenne à Paris.[17] Il est curieux de constater que Mersenne ignore l'un des pseudonymes d'Hevelius et qu'il demande des précisions à ce sujet.[18] Par ailleurs, on sait comment Aristarque a servi de paravent à Roberval et comment Mersenne a été mêlé à toute l'affaire[19].... Quand on feuillette la table onomastique qui se trouve à la fin de chaque volume de la *Correspondance de Mersenne*, on est étonné de voir l'abondance des noms cités (et identifiés pour la plupart) et la variété de la documentation que cela suppose. Autant que possible, les noms sont donnés dans leur langue originale. C'est ainsi qu'on préfère, pour les identifications, dire Höwelcke, plutôt qu'Hevelius; Dal Pozzo, plutôt que Dupuy; Van der Put, plutôt que Puteanus; Patrizzi, plutôt que Patricius. Quand il y a un double nom, on essaie de choisir le nom le plus courant, par exemple Peiresc, plutôt que Fabri de Peiresc; Montmort, plutôt que Habert de Montmort; Cherbury, plutôt que Herbert de Cherbury. En cas de pseudonyme, on renvoie au nom de famille quand on le connaît: ainsi François de la Noue, au lieu de Flaminius; Francowitz, au lieu de Flacius Illyricus; Bartolomeo Sacchi, au lieu de Platina.

4º — C'est aussi un usage suivi par les différents éditeurs de la *Correspondance* que de donner *in extenso*[20] le *titre* des ouvrages cités dans le texte de l'une des lettres ou même auxquels il est fait allusion. C'est le moyen de vivre vraiment avec les savants du XVIIe siècle, savoir ce qui les intéresse, ce qu'ils adoptent, ce qu'ils rejettent. Dans chacune de ses lettres, à tous ses correspondants, Mersenne raconte ce que l'on publie, il cite des titres, parle des auteurs, de la vente, des éditions successives ... En retour, il demande le même service à ses amis. Il veut savoir ce que l'on produit en Italie,[21] en Suisse,[22] en Pologne,[23] en Hollande,[24] dans les provinces de France. Et dès qu'il a reçu des précisions, il les communique aussitôt à d'autres amis.

5º — De tels renseignements doivent être commentés par des notes, parfois même par ce que nous appelons des *éclair-*

cissements, sortes de commentaires que l'on insère à la fin de la lettre comme de petits articles de quelques lignes à quelques pages. Il existe plusieurs ouvrages de références bibliographiques concernant le XVIIe siècle. Mais, après la consultation des volumes de la *Correspondance de Mersenne*, on est étonné de constater combien leurs notes ou leurs éclaircissements apportent de nouvelles précisions auxquelles, jusqu'ici, on n'avait pas songé. C'est ainsi par exemple que ces notes ou éclaircissements permettent en 1644 d'étudier le fameux voyage de Mersenne en Italie, sa rencontre avec Torricelli, son amitié avec Ricci ou Cavalieri. En 1645, des questions bibliques et théologiques. En 1645 et 1646, les problèmes de la cycloïde et l'*Aristarchus* de Roberval. En 1647 et 1648, les expériences sur le vide. De telle questions sont trop importantes pour qu'on ne s'y arrête pas, assez longuement parfois, par la rédaction de certains commentaires qui renverront le lecteur aux différentes étapes de recherches et aux résultats spectaculaires.

Ces études de noms, d'ouvrages, de renseignements de toutes sortes supposent une solide formation de base: les langues anciennes, les langues modernes, la connaissance de la théologie, des questions mathématiques, musicales, optiques, etc. Mais cette formation de base ne peut suffire: il faut sans cesse recourir aux textes, ceux des lettres bien sûr, mais aussi ceux des ouvrages du temps. Il faut se mettre dans l'atmosphère du XVIIe siècle, vivre et travailler comme travaillaient alors tant de savants et de chercheurs. Et quand on croit avoir trouvé une explication, il faut avoir l'humilité d'accepter une contradiction ou un refus de la part des lecteurs ou de soi-même.

Nous en arrivons maintenant à quelques questions très pratiques qu'il nous faut examiner. Le texte des lettres se présente dans la *Correspondance* pour plus de la moitié des cas en latin. D'autres lettres sont écrites en français, en italien, en anglais, en hollandais.... Certains passages sont en grec, d'autres en hébreu. Doit-on traduire en français tous ces textes? — Pour le latin, l'attitude des éditeurs n'a pas changé: ils savent que leurs lecteurs sont très cultivés et que, pour la plupart, ils connaissent au moins des rudiments susceptibles du leur rendre un texte à peu près compréhensible. Aussi a-t-on décidé de ne pas traduire le latin. C'est seulement dans les cas les plus délicats qu'une note ou un éclaircissement vient aider l'utilisateur. Pour le grec et l'hébreu, nettement moins employés, il y a parfois des traductions ou au moins des indications. Les textes en néerlandais ont été surtout rédigés par les maîtres-canonniers qui, sur la demande de Mersenne et grâce à l'appui de Constantin Huygens, faisaient des expériences de tir à l'armée: les textes, le plus souvent, ont été traduits en français. En revanche, au début de la collection, les langues modernes n'étaient pas traduites. Pourtant, à la demande de plusieurs lecteurs, les textes en italien sont traduits à partir du tome XIII et les textes en anglais à partir du tome XIV par les professeurs Speziali et Gabbey.

Restent certains détails à examiner: celui des caractères d'imprimerie. Pour l'ensemble de la collection, la typographie reste la même. Cependant à partir du tome V (1959), le travail de composition a été confié à la maison Darantiere de Dijon[25] qui, grâce au choix de ses caractères en monotypie et au soin de ses spécialistes, présente une édition de tout premier ordre. Les lettres de Mersenne ou à Mersenne sont écrites en caractères plus gros;[26] les autres lettres en caractères plus petits;[27] les éclaircissements sont en caractères plus gros[28] que les notes;[29] les variantes et les traductions[30] se différencient du reste du texte, ainsi que les chapeaux[31] et les références.[32] Cette variété et l'aération de l'ensemble rendent attrayantes lecture ou consultation.

Toutes les remarques que j'ai soumises jusqu'ici à votre sagacité s'appliquent à toute la collection de la *Correspondance de Mersenne* depuis le tome I jusqu'au tome XIV inclusivement. Deux volumes restent à paraître: le tome XV, presque terminé et concernant l'année 1647; le tome XVI, concernant l'année 1648, date de la mort de Mersenne.

A ce moment, va se poser la question des tables.... Jusqu'ici chaque volume se terminait par une table chronologique des lettres, une table alphabétique des correspondants, un index des noms de personne; au début du volume: une table des planches avec explication; à partir du volume XIII, une table des éclaircissements. Grâce à l'activité du Centre Alexandre Koyré,[33] des tables et un index cumulatif (102 pages) avaient paru en 1972: il s'appliquaient aux 10 premiers tomes de la *Correspondance* et fournissent encore actuellement un instrument de travail incomparable. Mais dès la fin du tome XVI, et dans un tome XVII, il sera opportun de dresser de nouvelles tables et, cette fois, pour la collection entière. A côté de l'index onomastique, prendra place un *index rerum* qui permettra de retrouver facilement les principaux sujets traités.

S'il fallait résumer les propos que je viens de développer devant vous, je crois qu'il faudrait se rendre compte de l'objectif que se sont proposé les éditeurs de la *Correspondance*: ils ont essayé de faire comprendre aux lecteurs du XXe siècle le rythme de la pensée du XVIIe siècle. A cause de documents de premier ordre, je veux dire les lettres de nos personnages, ils ont tenté d'expliquer, grâce aux textes et aux commentaires, comment Mersenne pouvait être l'héritier de ses devanciers les plus lointains, comment il a pu les dépasser par lui-même ou grâce à ses amis, comment, par sa clairvoyance et par les résultats de son travail, il annonce notre science actuelle. C'est l'un des buts de l'Histoire des Sciences que de saisir sur le vif le développement des recherches scientifiques au cours de l'Histoire. Avec Mersenne qui résuma toute une époque et qui centralisa tant de renseignements, nous arrivons au centre même d'une intense activité intellectuelle, celle de la première partie du XVIIe siècle.[34]

NOTES

1. *Correspondance de Mersenne, t. 1*, p xxiv.
2. "Nouvelles de la République des Lettres," 1981, n° I, pp 24–59.
3. *Corresp., t. XIII*, pp 68–71.

4. *Bibl. nat.*, f. fr., nouv. acq. 6204, 6205, 6206.
5. Libri (1803–69) fut naturalisé français et nommé membre de l'Institut en 1833, Professeur à la Faculté des Sciences en 1834, chargé en 1841, par ordonnance, du catalogue général pour la France de tous les manuscrits. Ses dépradations furent découvertes quand il voulut vendre sa coupable collection. Voir L. Delisle, *Catalogue des Manuscrits des fonds Libri et Barrois* (Paris: Champion, 1888), pp xxxvi, 330 — Libri n'eut pas entre ses mains le 4ᵉ volume dont arbogast (1759–1803) signale déjà la perte.
6. Voir par exemple *Correspondance, t. II*, p 24; *t. VI*, p 339; *t.IX*, p 300.
7. P. Dibon, *Inventaire de la Correspondance d'A. Rivet* (La Haye: Nijhoff, 1971), p 403, s.v. Mersenne.
8. *Oeuvres de Descartes*, Adam-Tannery, Nouv. éd. (Paris: C.N.R.S. — Vrin, 1969), *t. I*, p xxv.
9. *Ibid*, p xviii.
10. *Opere di Ev. Torricelli* ... a cura di G. Loria e G. Vassura, *vol III* (Faenza: Montanari, 1919), pp 256–7. *Corresp. t. XIII*, p 328.
11. Voir *Corresp. t. XV* et *XVI, in loco*.
12. *Corresp. t. XIV*, p 398.
13. *Corresp. t. XIII*, p 64.
14. *Corresp. t. XIV*, pp 208–9.
15. *Corresp. t. XIII*, p 46.
16. *Corresp. t. XIV*, p 434.
17. *Corresp. t. X*, p 723.
18. Voir *Corresp. t. XV*.
19. *Corresp. t. XIV*, p 66 sq.
20. C'est à dire: Nom de l'auteur; titre complet (s'il est vraiment trop long: les mots essentiels); lieu d'édition ou d'impression; éditeur; année; format; nombre des pages et, si possible, des illustrations.
21. *Corresp. t. XIV*, pp 123, 476, etc.
22. *Ibid*, p 209.
23. *Corresp. t. XIII*, p 544.
24. *Ibid*, pp 39, 105, 121, etc.
25. Auparavant, c'étaient les Presses Universitaires de France (Paris) qui s'étaient chargées des travaux d'éditions et d'imprimerie.
26. 71–13 corps 12.
27. 44–11 corps 12.
28. 44–10 corps 11.
29. 44–8 corps 8 (sur deux colonnes de 11 cicéros).
30. 44–9 corps 9.
31. 44–10 corps 11.
32. 72–10 corps 11.
33. Sous la direction de M. René Taton.
34. Epoque où grâce à Mersenne et à ses contemporains, commença à se former l'internationale *République des Lettres*.

The Thrice-Revealed Newton
I. Bernard Cohen

1. THE FIRST REVELATION

I have entitled my presentation "the thrice-revealed Newton"
because we have learned about Isaac Newton in a succession
of three revelations. First of all, there was the Newton revealed by his own choice of material to be published. For Newton,
"published" has the sense of being made public, that is, it includes distribution of long-hand copies and is not limited to
works put into print. In Newton's lifetime, this revelation
was made through the *Principles*, the *Opticks*, his famous letter on the production of prismatic colors and the nature of
white light, certain tracts on mathematics, and his study of
The Chronology of Ancient Kingdoms Amended.[1] Newton
thus showed himself to the world as a mathematician and
mathematical physicist and astronomer, a master of experiment, and a careful reasoner about questions of chronology

and succession related to Scripture. There was also circulated a paper entitled "De natura acidorum," which revealed some of Newton's chemical (and possibly alchemical) interests and speculations.[2] But the major image that Newton showed to the world was that of the prince of reason in an age in which reason was highly esteemed.

The major revelation of Newton the scientist was made in his celebrated *Mathematical Principles of Natural Philosophy*. Here was a cold, formal, logical presentation, in which — apparently — a rational system of the world was deduced by logic and mathematics from a series of first principles or "axioms" which Newton designated as "Axioms, or Laws of Motion," following upon a series of Definitions.[3] Second to the *Principles* was the *Opticks*, a non-mathematical treatise on "The Reflections, Refractions, Inflections, and Colours of Light."[4] For about a century and a half, with a few exceptions,[5] the image of Newton that dominated the thinking of men and women was that of a mathematician and physicist who was the highest representative of the Augustan Age, the Age of Reason.

This image of Newton was celebrated in verse, in sculpture, in painting. Newton was seen in the role of lawgiver of nature, or at least the agent who, by the exercise of his reason, had revealed nature's laws.[6] This was expressed succinctly in Alexander Pope's couplet:

Nature and Nature's laws lay hid in night;
God said, Let Newton be, and all was light.

For many people of that Augustan Age, the twin luminaries of reason were Isaac Newton and the philosopher of common sense, John Locke.[7] These were two heroes to Thomas Jefferson, who ordered portraits of them, along with a portrait of a third great Englishman, Francis Bacon, so that the three could adorn the walls of his study, as they do to this day.[8]

In order to present such an image of himself to the world, Newton had to make a very careful selection from among his writings or among the subjects of his interest, putting aside his explorations of theology, including interpretations of the prophecies in the Book of Revelation.[9] He had equally to conceal a long-abiding passion for alchemy[10] and his belief in priscan knowledge, a belief that much of the science that we know today was but a rediscovery of the wisdom known to ancient sages and seers.[11] On Newton's death, in 1727, the executors of his estate bundled up the manuscripts on these strange or esoteric subjects and marked them with the words that still remain for all to see who study Newton's manuscripts in the Universtiy Library at Cambridge or in the library of King's College,[12] "Not fit to be printed."[13]

This side of Newton, however, could not be totally hidden. Although later generations of scientists and philosophers hailed Newton as a positivies,[14] as a hard-headed scientist, there are traces to be found in the writings that Newton allowed to be published of the "other" Newton, even though our complete knowledge of the "other" Newton had to await a second and even a third revelation. For instance, the so-called positivist Newton says plainly in the General Scholium, which he wrote for the second edition of the *Principles* (1713),[15]

Hitherto I have explained the phenomena of the heavens and of our sea by the force of gravity, but I have not yet assigned a cause to gravity.... It is enough that gravity really exists and acts according to the laws set forth by us and can produce all the motions of the heavenly bodies and of our sea.

But the non-positivist[16] Newton says in that very same General Scholium that to discuss God "on the basis of phenomena belongs to experimental philosophy," a sentence somewhat toned down in the third edition (1726) to read that a discussion of God on the basis of phenomena belongs to "natural philosophy." And in the *Opticks*, in the queries added to the Latin edition of 1706 and printed in the second English edition of 1717/18,[17] Newton twice called space the sensorium of God, which — after the book had been printed — he slightly toned down in one place (but not in the other) by adding the Latin word "tanquam" — meaning "as it were."[18]

That Newton was concerned with theological questions, and that he was concerned with them in direct relation to his science, was also made apparent by other portions of the *Principles* and the *Opticks*. For example, in the first edition of the *Principles*, Newton refers to God's wisdom in creating the planets of such relative masses and densities that those which are nearest to the sun could best withstand the sun's heat.[19] And in the second edition of the *Principles* the concluding General Scholium (to which I have just referred) begins with a somewhat similar argument: that the solar system, with the planets all encircling the sun in approximately a single plane, all moving in the same direction, and with their satellites similarly arranged, could not come into being without the active intervention of a divine being.[20] Although we tend to concentrate on the penultimate paragraph of the General Scholium, in which Newton seems almost to argue like a positivist and where we find his famous slogan, *Hypotheses non fingo* ("I feign [or frame][21] no hypotheses"), most of that General Scholium, some 80% or so, is devoted to the being, attributes, and name of God.

In the *Opticks*, in the later versions, in both the Latin edition of 1706 and the English edition of 1717/18, Newton not only talks about the way in which God created the world in terms of indivisible, non-wearing, everlasting atomic particles, but discusses the relation of science and morality, the corruptions of the sons of Noah, and other questions of a theological nature — not all of which are directly related to science.[22] For the cognoscenti, there were also references in the *Opticks* to nature's delight in making transmutations,[23] which may possibly have been read as a hint concerning the great man's interest in alchemy, the science of transmutation. It must be admitted, however, that Newton also uses the word transmutation for the changes that occur constantly around us by natural processes, and even for certain changes that occur in projective geometry, i.e., the "transmutation" of geometric figures.[24] The third and final book of Newton's *Principles* (1687) opens with a series of "Hypotheses," which in the later editions were largely divided into "Phenomena" and "Rules for Natural Philosophy";[25] the third "Hypothesis"[26] stated that "all matter can be transformed into matter of any other kind and successively undergo all the intermediate stages of qualities."[27] It must be said at once, however, that this particular statement was given by Newton without explanation; it was not really used in the rest of Book Three of the *Principles*, of which it was part of the introductory section.[28] Furthermore, it was labeled "Hypothesis III," which could have indicated that it was introduced for discussion as a hypothesis and was not necessarily a firm statement of Newton's own belief.[29]

We now know, however, that during the 1690's Newton planned to add certain additional scholiums to the third book of his *Principles*, in which he would give rein to some of his extravagant and certainly non-positivistic ideas. In part, he would include here some extracts from the *De rerum natura* of the Roman poet Lucretius and would also explain his idea that the ancient sages had a knowledge of nature which included even the law of universal gravity.[30] But apparently he thought better of this idea, and that revelation was made only about 300 years later, when his manuscript annotations in preparation for a new edition of the *Principles* were discovered and published.[31]

Newton's *Chronology of Ancient Kingdoms Amended* was circulated by Newton, but not intended to be printed.[32] Yet soon this work was in general circulation and did get into print.[33] It is not a very daring book for a rationalist or positivist. In developing his subject, Newton did assume that — among other things — the voyage of the "good ship Argo" was a real event and that one could believe all the accounts of the Argonauts and their search for the Golden Fleece, as reported by Apollonius of Rhodes, and similar kinds of events of the past. On this basis Newton essentially attempted to make a rational reconstruction of past events. He assumed that the precession of the equinoxes has been constant over the ages; he found in the literature of the past certain statements which he took as evidence of the appearance (visibility and position) of constellations and consequently as a basis for computing the dates of those alleged celestial observations. This is, in short, to some degree, a "scientific chronology" based on clearly stated hypotheses or assumptions. The point is that this endeavor is based on rational procedures.[34] The only part of such an analysis which would make us question its being worthy of the author of the great *Principles* or the *Opticks* would be the degree of Newton's credulity about what he assumes to have been actual historical events. Furthermore, we might be a little astonished that the prince of rationalism and the greatest scientist of his age should have devoted so much of his time and energy to the study of biblical history and the annals of ancient history, which — by comparison — would seem to us to have been a somewhat trivial occupation.

Newton's anti-Trinitarian views, on the other hand, were more carefully kept private.[35] The nearest to a "public" work relating to interpretation of Scripture, as opposed to purely chronological aspects of Scripture, was his study of the Book of Revelation, published shortly after his death.[36] It may be pointed out, however, that in Newton's day it would not have seemed unusual for a mathematical scientist to occupy himself with this subject. There was, in fact, that prior example of John Napier, Laird of Merchiston, known to us as the inventor of logarithms, who also produced a lengthy treatise on the Book of Revelation.[37]

In this work, Newton's aim was to interpret the prophecies to find out what they meant, but — as Frank Manuel has shown[38] — stopping short of actually making predictions of the future.[39] In evaluating this work, we must remember that in those days in Britain there was produced an enormous mass of literature concerning prophecy.[40] In the fourth decade of the 17th century, a Cambridge man, Joseph Mede of Christ's, had invented a rather new way of reading the prophetic literature, producing an innovation in method that Manuel has likened to a Copernican revolution[41] and that his contemporary "admirers glorified as equal in importance to Aristotle's syllogistic reasoning."[42] Newton's method of studying prophecy depended greatly on the work of Mede. I shall not go into the details of the method,[43] but it should be noted that Newton did not proceed by attempting a mystical union with the authors of the prophetic texts. For the most part his method was based on rational procedures and had the appearance of a "scientific" inquiry. Manuel has noted[44] that some Cambridge drafts of this work "used formal scientific" headings like 'Propositiones' and 'Lemmata'." This "scientific" aspect of Newton's work is plainly displayed in a general introduction to one of the Keynes manuscripts in King's College, Cambridge, entitled "The First Book Concerning the Language of the Prophets" (complete in itself in 152 pages; 50,000 words). Here Newton explains his method.

He that would understand a book written in a strange language must first learn the language, and if he would understand it well must learn the language perfectly. Such a language was that wherein the Prophets wrote, and the want of sufficient skill in that language is the main reason why they are so little understood. John did not write in one language, Daniel in another, Isaiah in a third, and the rest in others peculiar to themselves, but they all write in one and the same mystical language ... [which], so far as I can find, was as certain and definite in its signification as is the vulgar language of any nation....[45]

This is the basic premise of the work. Next Newton explains that "it is only through want of skill therein that Interpreters so frequently turn the Prophetic types and phrases to signify whatever their fancies and hypotheses lead them to." As with Cartesian philosophical romances, it was owing to ignorance that hypotheses took the place of correct explanations based on fact. The main procedural principle was stated as follows:

The Rule I have followed has been to compare the several mystical places of scripture where the same prophetic phrase or type is used, and to fix such a signification to that phrase as agrees best with all the places: ... and, when I had found the necessary significations, to reject all others as the offspring of luxuriant fancy, for no more significations are to be admitted for true ones than can be proved.

This statement sounds so much like the Rules at the beginning of Book Three of the *Principles* that it may well serve to illustrate the essential oneness of Newton's thought. It embodies the proper approach of a man who believes in the experimental (empirical) philosophy, and we shall see that a similar point of view may be found in Newton's studies of alchemy.

The published book of *Observations upon the Prophecies of Daniel and the Apocalypse of St. John*[46] deals with this same problem of "the Prophetic Language" — a "figurative language" used by the Prophets and "taken from the analogy between the world natural, and an empire or kingdom considered as a world politic." Essentially the whole matter turns on Daniel's prophecy concerning the Messiah, and the preliminary prophetic statements about an "Image composed of four Metals" and a stone which broke "the four Metals to pieces." These are the four nations successively ruling the earth (*viz* the people of Babylonia, the Persians, the Greeks, and the Romans"). The four nations are represented again in the "four Beasts." Reading through Newton's text is an exercise in history and a rather dull one. Here is no ecstasy of a mystic St Teresa or St John of the Cross, but a seemingly endless parade of dated events, lists of kings, battles, and successions, and an attempt to place all of them into a chronological frame that is more reminiscent of Newton's own *Chronology of Ancient Kingdoms Amended* than of the mystical writings of a Boehme. "The folly of Interpreters," says Newton, has been "to foretel times and things by this Prophecy, as if God designed to make them Prophets." This was, however, far from God's intent, according to Newton, for the prophecies were meant by God "not to gratify men's curiosities by enabling them to foreknow things" but rather to stand as witnesses to God's providence when "after they were fulfilled they might be interpreted by the event." Surely, he said, "the event of things predicted many ages before, will then be a convincing argument that the world is governed by providence." Nor is the *Observations* free from reference to Newton's favorite themes of the corruption of scripture and the corruption of Christianity.[47]

Newton died intestate in March 1727. Since he never married and had no children there inevitably arose a quarrel among his surviving relatives over the division of his estate — which we know amounted to "a considerable fortune."[48] Newton's papers were inventoried and evaluated for the heirs, and it was agreed that "only the Chronology & Prophecies [were] fitt to be appraised" — the value of £250 was set for the Chronology "& no value upon the Prophecies they being imperfect."[49] Thomas Pellet, a Fellow of the Royal Society, gave his own examination, and most of Newton's manuscripts to this day bear his annotation, to which I have referred earlier, "Not fit to be printed." Very likely — as Whiteside reminds us — this remark has nothing to do with what we would consider the scholarly or intrinsic intellectual value of Newton's manuscripts, papers, or notebooks, but rather relates strictly to their "fitness" as complete works ready for printing and accordingly having monetary value.

A description of the evaluation of Newton's papers was written by John Conduitt, the husband of Newton's niece and Newton's successor at the Mint. Conduitt hoped to preserve as intact as possible all the remaining writings of the great man into whose family he had married. He relates that, according to Dr Pellet, there were only five works which were possibly in a state "fitt to be printed."[50] These included the *Chronology of Ancient Kingdoms Amended*, sold for £350 and printed for J. Tonson, the Strand bookseller; what was described as "A Mathematical tract De Motu Corporum," sold to Tonson for £31-10 and printed under the editorship of John Conduitt with the confusing title *De mundi systemate*;[51] Newton's work on the prophecies, published under the title *Observations upon the Prophecies of Daniel and the Apocalypse of St. John* (printed in 1733 by "J.Darby and T. Browne in Bartholomew Close"); a set of "Paradoxical Questions concerning Athanasius" which remains unpublished to this day, although extracts were published by David Brewster in his two-volume biography of Newton in 1855,[52] further extracts published by H. McLachlan in 1950,[53] and further extracts by F.E. Manuel in 1963;[54] and, finally, what is described as "an Imperfect Mathematical tract," probably — according to Whiteside[55] — a combination of "the unfinished 1666 English and 1671 Latin fluxional tracts ... which Horsley was to find packaged together in 1777."

Conduitt attempted to prepare a biography of Newton, of which we have many fragmentary drafts, containing extracts from letters and biographical accounts which Conduitt solicited from many of those who knew Newton; these are precious documents for any biographer.[56] But Conduitt never took care to order, to catalogue in detail, or even to find a proper repository for the unpublished manuscripts, notebooks, correspondence, and other documents belonging to Newton.[57] His wife Catherine, Newton's niece,[58] was especially anxious to publish the papers of her famous uncle dealing with problems of religion and chronology; her will contains a codicil in which her executor is directed to "lay all the Tracts relating to Divinity before Dr. Sykes ... in hopes he will prepare them for the press...." Further, "I ordain" that "all of them ... shall be printed and published, so as they be done with care and exactness." She noted that in relation to "whatever proffit may arise from the same, my dear Mr. Conduitt has given a bond of £2000 to be responsible to the seven nearest of kin to Sir Is. Newton." Therefore, she declared, "the papers must be carefully kept" and "no copys may be taken and printed." Additionally, "Dr. Sykes [is] desired to peruse them here, otherways if any accident comes to them the penalty of the Bond will be levy'd."[59] Apparently, "no new work of Isaac Newton's appeared in the stationers' catalogues"[60] until the Latin version of the 1671 fluxional tract was published fifty years later as part of the five-volume edition of Newton's *Opera* edited by Samuel Horsley.

John Conduitt died in May 1737, his wife Catherine in January 1739. Then Newton's papers passed to their daughter, who married John Wallop, who became Viscount Lymington when his father was created the first Earl of Portsmouth in 1743. These precious documents[61] remained in the Portsmouth family until, as we shall see, the "scientific portion" came to the University of Cambridge in the late 1880's and the rest were dispersed at public auction in the 1930's.

For various reasons, Horsley's five-volume edition of Newton's *Opera* does not contain any considerable new manuscript material, an exception being the selections from Newton's correspondence with Oldenburg which appear in Volume Four.[62] Horsley apparently was allowed to see the family collection too late to make any extensive use of it, for "his first volume [was] already in press in London and anxiously awaited by his subscribers."[63] Accordingly, in the mathematical field he only "suitably improved certain texts already scheduled for publication by collating them with the manuscript (notably emending the text of the "Geometria analytica,") which he had previously derived from two inferior copies, one indeed derivative from the other...." A creative editor by the standards of his time, Horsley did make divisions, for example into chapters and paragraphs, and he provided valuable annotations for his edition of the *Opticks*, in which he indicated important changes in the queries from edition to edition, which have stood until our own times as the only major attempt to delineate the development of Isaac Newton's ideas on the nature of light, atoms, aether, particulate forces, and chemistry, as expressed in the queries.

2. THE SECOND REVELATION

The works in print by the end of the decade following Newton's death provided the world with an image of Newton and a knowledge of his mathematical and scientific acheivements that remained essentially unaltered for a century or more. The second revelation really began in about the middle of the 19th century, with the publication in 1855 of the two volumes of David Brewster's massive biography of Newton, with its extensive appendixes containing new texts published from manuscript sources.

Brewster's biography was only one of four important works published in the middle of the 19th century, each containing new material based upon manuscripts relating to Isaac Newton. The first was a collection by S.P Rigaud (1838) containing documents chiefly relating to Newton's *Principles* with an important introduction. Rigaud published for the first time the text of the tract *De motu* which Newton wrote out after Halley's famous visit in 1684 and which is the first organized and complete statement of his analysis of elliptical orbital motion and his proof that if elliptical orbits result from the action of a central force on a body, the force must vary inversely as the square of the distance.[64] Rigaud also began a two-volume collection of correspondence in the possession of the Earl of Macclesfield, which contains valuable correspondence by and to Isaac Newton and the correspondence of others which is related to Newton. This collection, begun and organized by Rigaud, was finally published by his son in 1841, but an index was added by Augustus De Morgan only a number of years later (1862). A third work, one of the most valuable contributions to Newtonian scholarship ever produced, was the edition in 1850 of the letters which passed between Newton and Cotes (who prepared the second edition of the *Principles* under Newton's direction) and which are preserved in a large volume in the Trinity College Library. This exemplary work, with very illuminating and important notes by the editor, Joseph Edleston, is preceded by an extremely valuable detailed chronology of Newton's life, filled in with important documentary materials, such as Newton's entrances and exits from Trinity College according to the Register Book.

These three works filled out many details concerning Newton's scientific thought, but they do not really constitute a major revelation about Newton. That was reserved for David Brewster's two-volume biography (1855) with extensive documentary appendices.[65] It has been assumed, as L.T. More (a later biographer of Newton) asserted, that Brewster "made a very considerable use of Conduitt's manuscripts and of abstracts from Newton's correspondence, and some use of the mathematical notes and papers [but] used his discretion in extracting and in omitting many important documents which seemed to him not advantageous to Newton's reputation.[66] But Whiteside has shown that "Brewster was apparently never allowed unrestricted access to the Portsmouth manuscripts but limited almost wholly to the selection of biographically pertinent material, letters and papers selected for him by [Henry] Fellowes."[67] Brewster himself, as Whiteside has noted, is rather explicit on this matter:

In this examination [of "the large mass of papers which Sir Isaac had left behind him"] our attention was particularly directed to such letters and papers as were calculated to throw light upon his early and academical life, and, with the assistance of Mr. Fellowes, who copied for me several important documents, I was enabled to collect many valuable materials unknown to preceding biographers....

The materials ... are of great value; and in so far as Mr. H.A. Fellowes and I could make an abstract of these and other manuscripts during a week's visit at [Hurstbourne] Park, I have availed myself of them in composing the first volume of this work, which was printed before the papers themselves came into my hands.[68]

For the second volume, Brewster says that "I had the good fortune to obtain from the Earl of Portsmouth the collection of manuscripts and correspondence which the late Mr. H.A. Fellowes had examined and arranged as peculiarly fitted to throw light on the Life and Discoveries of Sir Isaac."[69]

Brewster has often been castigated for the fact that he so adulated his hero that he referred to Newton even in his school days as "young Sir Isaac," even though Newton was not knighted until old age. He was also criticized for having again and again called Newton the "High Priest of Science." Yet it must be kept in mind that the phrase "High Priest of Science" was not of Brewster's own invention but was merely taken over by him from what is perhaps the first true biography of Newton, by William Stukeley,[70] who wrote a short version to be used by Conduitt in preparing his own biography of Newton. Stukeley did a considerable amount of research, it should be noted, and he even submitted Newton to an oral-history interview, thereby inaugurating that practice in the history of science. Stukeley relates that when he asked Newton how he came to think of the law of universal gravity, Newton replied that it was while sitting in a garden, much as he was while having tea with Stukeley.[71] Apparently, therefore, Newton himself was the originator of the apple story.[72] I have long considered that Stukeley's actions may serve as an object lesson to all historians of science. He had a unique opportunity to ask Newton: And what were the circumstances? How did the falling of an apple bring this idea into your mind? In what year did this occur? What had you been thinking about at that time? But Stukeley merely went on to the next subject.[73]

What is probably of the greatest significance in Brewster's two-volume life is the fact that for the first time in print some real indication was given of Newton's actual manuscript writings on theology and alchemy. With regard to the latter, Brewster was quite shocked to find that the "High Priest of Science" not only had been a devotee of alchemy, but had copied out (in his own hand) works that Brewster could only describe as foul and characterized by charlatanry.[74] He also wanted it believed that one of Newton's major aims in studying alchemy was to discredit the pretensions of that subject. Yet, for all that, Brewster had to admit: "There is no problem of more difficult solution than that which relates to the belief in alchemy, and to the practice of its arts, by men of high character and lofty attainments."[75] Brewster pointed out that there are remarkable changes in nature, such as that gold and silver and other metals "may be extracted from transparent crystals, which scarcely differ in their appearance from a piece of common salt or a bit of sugar-candy."[76] He also said that it is astonishing that aluminum "can be extracted from clay," or that "lights of the most dazzling colours can be obtained from the combustion of colourless salts," or that "gas, giving the most brilliant light, resides in a lump of coal or a block of wood." Need we then wonder, says Brewster, "that the most extravagant expectations were entertained of procuring from the basest materials the precious metals and the noblest gems."[77]

But how really could men of such rational character and scientific soundness — Newton, Boyle, and Locke — give their time and intellectual energy to the study of alchemy? Of course, said Brewster, the "ambition neither of wealth nor of praise prompted their studies." He pompously declared: "We may safely say that a love of truth alone, a desire to make new discoveries in chemistry, and a wish to test the extraordinary pretensions of their predecessors and their contemporaries, were the only motives by which they were actuated."[78] Thus, he continued, "insofar as Newton's inquiries were limited to the transmutation and multiplication of metals, and even to the discovery of the universal tincture, we may find some apology for his researches."[79] But Brewster quite frankly admitted his own complete inability to "understand how a mind of such power, and so nobly occupied with the abstractions of geometry, and the study of the material world, could stoop to be even the copyist of the most contemptible alchemical poetry, and the annotator of a work, the obvious production of a fool and a knave." Yet he was forced to explain:"Such, however, was the taste of the century in which Newton lived, and, when we denounce the mental epidemics of the past age, we may find some palliation of them in those of our own times."[80] Brewster sadly admitted the fact and there was nothing he could do about it, but he did conclude with the expression of a pious belief that "there is reason to believe" that Newton "had learned to have but little confidence even in the humbler department of the multiplication of metals." Forsooth!

Brewster was honest enough to admit that he had seen in Newton's own handwriting *The Metamorphoses of the Planets* by John De Monte Snyders together with a key to it, plus "numerous pages of alchemist poetry," chiefly from Norton's *Ordinal* and Basil Valentine's *Mystery of the Microcosm*. He also had seen a copy of *Secrets Revealed, Or an Open Entrance to the Shut Palace of the King*," covered with notes in Sir Isaac's hand, in which great changes are made upon the language and meaning of the thirty-five chapters of which it consists."[81] And so on. Brewster did not hide from the world the fact that Newton made "copious extracts from the writings of the alchemists of all ages," and that he produced a "very large *Index Chemicus* and *Supplementum*

Indicis Chemici, with minute references to the different subjects to which they relate."[82] Who could doubt that Newton had been a serious student of alchemy, even making alchemical experiments during his most creative period of life, the 1680's, while writing the *Principles?*

With regard to theology, the problem was somewhat different for Brewster. He had earlier published a one-volume work in which he asserted that Newton was certainly a believer in the Trinity and orthodox.[83] But now, having had access to the manuscripts, from which he quoted at length, he had to tone down his earlier assertion. Painful as it must have been for him, Brewster did print a number of texts and extracts from the manuscripts which make it obvious that Newton had strong Unitarian or Arian leanings.[84]

On the more positive side, Brewster assembled sound evidence to prove that Biot had made an error in assuming that Newton's interest in theology arose in his old age, when he was in his dotage and unable to do any more creative work in mathematics and the sciences. And Brewster made available an enormous amount of new documentary information concerning Newton's creative scientific career, the development and reception of his ideas and their philosophical implications, and the facts of Newton's life. But although Brewster did show that there was substance in the rumors concerning Newton's pursuit of alchemy and interest in theology, this second revelation did not inspire scholars to attempt to make a further study of Newton's manuscripts (which might have proved impossible in any event). Thus Brewster's biography remained the standard source for knowledge of Newton's religious beliefs until the third revelation, which has only occurred in the last decades.

3. BETWEEN THE SECOND AND THIRD REVELATIONS

A number of significant events occured between the second and third revelations. In July 1872, two eminent Cambridge mathematicians, Professor John Couch Adams and Professor Sir George G. Stokes, went to Hurstbourne Park "to look over the Newton papers"[85] and to report back to the university concerning them. When Adams and Stokes saw the vast size and variety of the collection, they quickly realized that they could not study these manuscripts in the time of a brief visit. Lord Portsmouth graciously agreed to send all of the papers, including "two *copies* of the Principia 1st & 2nd Editions corrected by Newton" and "a Number of Fragments relating to Mathematics," plus "some very interesting letters from Eminent Men to Newton" and "memoranda Books &c relating to personal matters."[86] Lord Portsmouth made it clear, however, that he was only "willing to *lend*" most of these items. It was his "wish," he said, "to advance the interests of science by placing these Papers at the service of the University, but [he concluded] I would rather cut my hand off than sever my connection with Newton which is the proudest Boast of my Family."[87]

It was evidently the wish of the Earl of Portsmouth "to make ... over to the University" the papers and correspondence relating to science, since he believed "that these would find a more appropriate home in the Library of Newton's own University than in that of a private individual."[87 a]

Newton's manuscripts, correspondence, and papers were studied in Cambridge over the next 16 years by a syndicate composed of Adams and Stokes plus the Reverend Henry Richards Luard (Registrary of the University and Perpetual Curate of Great St Mary's) and George Downing Liveing (of St John's College, professor of chemistry). This syndicate produced a catalogue of the collection[88] after they had made a laborious examination and classification. They divided the collection into two parts, half of which was given by the Earl of Portsmouth to the University Library, where it is usually referred to as the Portsmouth Collection,[89] and the remainder returned to the Earl. The syndicate noted that the job "has proved a lengthy and laborious business, as many of the papers were found to be in great confusion — mathematical notes being often inserted in the middle of theological treatises, and even numbered leaves of MSS. having got out of order. Moreover a large portion of the collection has been grievously damaged by fire and damp. The correspondence, however, is in a very fair condition throughout, and had been arranged in an orderly manner."[90]

It should be noted that the catalogue covers the whole collection of Newton's books and papers, not merely the portion given to the University. The preface of 20 pages begins with a two-page summary of the history of the manuscripts and an account of the committee's activities, then devotes two pages to Newton's work on the lunar theory, two pages to Newton's work on refraction, half a page to the determination of "the form of the solid of least resistance," and two pages to the extensive manuscript materials relating to Newton's quarrel with Leibniz over priority in the invention of the calculus.[91] A whole page is devoted to an autobiographical statement about how Newton made his discoveries, and then there are brief notes concerning the manuscripts on alchemy and on historical and theological subjects, plus an appendix giving a sample of the riches of the collection.[92] While studying the collection, Adams and Luard made careful long-hand transcripts of many letters and documents which were intended to be returned to the Earl of Portsmouth.[93]

It might be supposed that the availability to scholars of this rich treasure of historical materials, the nature of which was made evident by the published catalogue, would have attracted a certain amount of scholarly attention. But for about half a century this great collection remained virtually unused in the University Library at Cambridge. We may agree with Whiteside that "inexplicably its contemporary impact was almost nil."[94] Perhaps the reason is that "no member of the cataloguing syndicate implemented the official report with an enlightening secondary study, historical or biographical, of any of the documents he had pondered over so long."

The literature of the history of science shows that during this period of a half-century, only one major use was made of the collection, by the historian of mathematics Walter William Rouse Ball. He published the results of a careful examination of Newton's unpublished manuscript (in the Portsmouth Collection) on the classification of cubic curves (1891) and also a brief but important critique of a manuscript of Newton on central forces (1892). He also published, from the manuscripts, an essay of Newton's on the role of mathematics in university education.[95] Additionally, he drew on the Newtonian manuscript corpus in preparing his important essay on the "genesis of the *Principia*."[96] Here, among other things, Rouse Ball included the text of Newton's tract *De motu*, which — as I have mentioned — had been published some 50 years earlier by Rigaud, from the version in the Royal Society. Whiteside found only two other serious users of the Portsmouth Collection prior to the 1930's.[97] Duncan C. Fraser published and analyzed some of Newton's papers on interpolation,[98] and a German scholar, Alexander Witting, "studied the fluxional manuscripts in Cambridge and prepared a preliminary report."[99] The latter undertook this work a few years before the 1914 war and, when the war was over, never returned to it.

In the 30's, Louis Trenchard More examined the papers in the Portsmouth Collection in the University Library and also had access to the papers still in the possession of the family. In the preface to his biography (1934), he expressed his gratitude "to Blanche, Lady Portsmouth, and to her nephew, Viscount Lymington, who, although I was then a stranger to them, sent their priceless collection in Hurstbourne Park to the British Museum in order that I might examine and use it at my leisure." Although More quoted some extracts from Newton's MS documents and notebooks, he apparently did not bother much with the large body of material assembled by Newton relating to alchemy. In his discussion of this subject, in fact, the only extracts he quoted are a letter from Newton to Oldenburg about Boyle's experiments (previously published in the works of Boyle and in Rigaud's two volumes of selections from the Macclesfield Collection) and a little over a page extracted from the published Query 31 of the *Opticks*. But More did state, unequivocally, "The fact of the matter is, Newton was an alchemist, and his major interest in chemistry, in his earlier years, centred in the possibility of transmuting metals." And he added that there was "a mystical strain" in Newton's "character which had been quite overlooked. It showed itself not only in his persistent reading of the esoteric formulae of the alchemists, but also in his sympathy for the philosophy of the Cambridge Platonists and in his extended interpretations of the prophecies of the Books of Daniel and of the Revelation."[100] More argued that "there can be no doubt that [Newton] not only seriously sought the transmutation of metals into gold and the universal panacea for disease and old age, but also believed them to be the chief goal of the chemist."[101] But More gave no idea of the vast extent of Newton's alchemical manuscripts, including his lengthy transcripts of writings on this subject, his attempt to catalogue the authors and to find out which were the best, and his efforts to find identities in language and expression among the many writers on the subject.

In a lengthy footnote occupying half a page, More[102] attacked the statement of Brewster that Newton's alchemy, as well as Boyle's and Locke's, was not of the kind "commencing in fraud and terminating in mysticism." And he indicated that Brewster had erred in stating that it had been "a love of truth alone" and "a wish to test the *extraordinary pretensions* of their predecessors and their contemporaries" that had provided "the only motives by which [Boyle, Newton, and Locke] were actuated."

More, however, did better with Newton's theology. In fact, More stated expressly:

What we can learn from the published theological works of Newton is obscured by his caution, a caution which must have been increased by the misfortunes of Whiston. When I was generously given permission to examine, and to make extracts from, the *Portsmouth Collection* I was particularly anxious to see whether the vexed question of his religious opinions could not be answered from the documents which Horsley and Brewster did not feel it wise to publish. And I think the answer can now be given.[103]

More concluded that Newton "was wholly committed, as was Milton, to the Protestant doctrine against the authority of the Church Councils." And he emphasized the fact that "personally, Newton was an Arian since he states definitely that the Father and the Son are not one substance; that the

Son was created and therefore of a different substance for, if they were of one substance then, the Father having created the substance of the Son, He must have created His own substance."[104] According to More, "Newton goes much farther than merely to deny the doctrine of consubstantiation. He had rationally adopted the Unitarian position that Jesus was sent by the Father into the world as a Prophet who differed from the other Prophets only in the immediacy of the message delivered to him." Yet, "like so may other Unitarians of the day, such as Locke, he ... makes a break between reason and practice, since he maintained his affiliation with the Church of England."[105] Clearly, save for an aspect of Newton's theological beliefs, More's biography did not substantially change our view of Newton. The third revelation had not yet occurred by the 1930's, despite a half-century of availability of the Portsmouth Collection.[105 a]

4. THE THIRD REVELATION

The first date in the third revelation is 1936. In that year, in order to pay the death duties, the family turned over the remaining mass of Newtonian manuscripts, annotated books, correspondence, notebooks, and personal memorabilia, including portraits and busts (but not the major portraits in oil) for public auction at Sotheby's. There were in the material put up for auction some three million words in Newton's autograph, according to the estimate of the cataloguer, and — shocking as it seems to us today — the total realized by this sale was a mere £9030–10s–0d, less than $30,000. The late A.N.L. Munby remarked that the sale did have at least one beneficial effect: the sale catalogue assembled by John Taylor.[106] This catalogue is a learned document, giving extensive extracts from many of the most important documents, and reproducing pages from a number of the major texts in facsimile. Here, for example, was startling and dramatic proof of the extent of Newton's involvement in alchemy.

As a result of the sale, Newton's manuscripts were literally scattered to the four corners of the earth and some have —

one hopes only temporarily — disappeared from sight altogether. Thanks to the foresight of Lord Keynes (the economist John Maynard Keynes),[107] a large number of Newton's major alchemical manuscripts and the materials assembled by John Conduitt for preparing a biography of Newton were put together in a single collection and returned to the University of Cambridge, permanently this time, in King's College Library. Also, thanks to the activities of a variety of interested parties, some of these important documents ended up in Trinity, which had already been given a major part of the books from Newton's personal library, some of them annotated in Newton's hand and others dog-eared — as was Newton's fashion — so that the corner of the page would point toward a place of interest.[108]

One of the effects of this sale was to call attention to the extent of Newton's still unpublished papers, but it must be confessed that there was not an immediate flurry of Newton scholarship. The reason is that many of Newton's papers had been purchased by dealers in books and manuscripts and were not available for study. Only gradually did they become concentrated in a few private collections and find their way into libraries where they could be studied. No doubt, interest in Newton and in his manuscripts would have been stimulated by the tercentenary of his birth (1942), but even that could not be properly celebrated until after the war.[109]

As everyone knows, since the 1950's, Newton scholarship has grown into what has become called a "Newton industry," although there has been no concerted effort to produce a standard and uniform edition of Newton's writings like the editions of Galileo, of Huygens, and (in progress) of Kepler. The Royal Society did undertake to produce an edition of Newton's correspondence, now complete in seven volumes, begun under the editorship of H.W. Turnbull, continued by J.F. Scott, and completed by A. Rupert Hall and Laura Tilling. Not only does this edition include letters written by Newton and received by him, but there is also a generous selection of manuscript documents relating to scientific and other questions by Newton and — in particular — by David Gregory, who made many memoranda after visiting Newton and seeing his manuscripts and work in progress. The most notable work of editing in Newtonian scholarship has been the magisterial *Mathematical Papers of Isaac Newton*, produced under the able editorship of D.T. Whiteside of Cambridge University, just completed in eight tremendous volumes. Here are assembled, ordered, and classified all of Newton's writings on — or related to — mathematics, together with historical, analytical, and interpretive commentaries and introductions that by themselves constitute one of the major contributions to the history of mathematics, the history of 17th-century science, and our understanding of Newton's development, Alexandre Koyré, Anne Whitman, and I assembled an edition of Newton's *Principles* that was based on a collation of the printer's MS, the three printed editions (1687, 1713, 1726), and two examples of the second and of the first editions containing Newton's MS revisions. This work is currently being supplemented by a new English version of Newton's *Principles* and of the *Essay on the System of the Universe*.[110] Two major jobs of editing Newton's writings are Henry Guerlac's forthcoming edition of the *Opticks* and Alan Shapiro's edition of the *Optical Lectures*. In 1962, A. Rupert and Marie Boas Hall brought out a major collection of *Unpublished Scientific Papers of Isaac Newton*, followed in 1965 by John Herivel's *The Background to Newton's "Principia,"* a substantial part of which was an edited anthology of MS writings of Isaac Newton. Newton's published *Papers & Letters on Natural Philosophy* were edited for publication in 1958 (second edition, 1978) by I.B. Cohen, assisted by R.E. Schofield. A large company of scholars have studied, edited, or published important manuscript material in books and articles. They include A. Rupert Hall and Marie Boas Hall, John W. Herivel, Frank Manuel, Henry Guerlac, J.E. McGuire, P.M. Rattansi, Alexandre Koyré, R.S. Westfall, Betty Jo Teeter Dobbs, Karin Figala, I.B. Cohen, Alan Shapiro, J.P. Lohne, and others. The effect of their writings cumulatively is to produce the third revelation of Newton.[110a]

The esoteric side of this thrice-revealed Newton was heralded in a famous lecture written by Lord Keynes and read by his brother, Sir Geoffrey, at the Newton Tercentenary Meetings at the Royal Society. A somewhat startled audience heard that Keynes — who had studied deeply the manuscripts that he had collected after the sale of the Portsmouth Papers — no longer believed in the traditional image of Newton but held that there was an altogether different Newton revealed by his secret papers. This now thrice-revealed Newton was described by Keynes as follows:

In the eighteenth century and since, Newton came to be thought of as the first and greatest of the modern age of scientists, a rationalist, one who taught us to think on the lines of cold and untinctured reason.

I do not see him in this light. I do not think that any one who has pored over the contents of that box which he packed up when he finally left Cambridge in 1696 and which, though partly dispersed, have come down to us, can see him like that. Newton was not the first of the age of reason. He was the last of the magicians, the last of the Babylonians and Sumerians, the last great mind which looked out on the visible and intellectual world with the same eyes as those who began to build our intellectual inheritance rather less than 10,000 years ago. Isaac Newton, a posthumous child born with no father on Christmas Day, 1642, was the last wonder-child to whom the Magi could do sincere and appropriate homage.

Then Keynes went on to say:

Why do I call him a magician? Because he looked on the whole universe and all that is in it *as a riddle*, as a secret which could be read by applying pure thought to certain evidence, certain mystic clues which God had laid about the world to allow a sort of philosopher's treasure hunt to the esoteric brotherhood. He believed that these clues were to be found partly in the evidence of the heavens and in the constitution of elements (and that is what gives the false suggestion of his being an experimental natural philosopher), but also partly in

certain papers and traditions handed down by the breth-
ren in an unbroken chain back to the original cryptic
revelation in Babylonia. He regarded the universe as a
cryptogram set by the Almighty — just as he himself
wrapt the discovery of the calculus in a cryptogram when
he communicated with Leibnitz. By pure thought, by
concentration of mind, the riddle, he believed, would be
revealed to the initiate.[111]

This was strong medicine and hard to take, for Keynes was
suggesting that Newton was to be understood through alchemy,
mystic philosophy, and the Hermetic tradition and not
through mathematics, physics, and astronomy, as had been
customary for three centuries.

Keynes's paper was written for a private group in Trinity
College, and there was no way of telling whether or not he
might have rewritten it for a public lecture to an international
company of scientists at the Royal Society's celebrations of
the tercentenary of Newton's birth. He died before the celebrations, and the original text — unrevised — was read by his
brother in 1946 and published as part of the proceedings in
1947. One year later, in 1948, A. Rupert Hall published what
may now be considered a landmark article on "Sir Isaac
Newton's Note-Book," the first scholarly article of the third
revelation to be based on the manuscripts.[112]

As far as I can tell, the next work to use Newton's unpublished MSS was the edition of Newton's *Theological Manuscripts* in 1950 by Herbert McLachlan, who drew upon the
riches of the Keynes Collection. In that same year, there was
published *A Descriptive Catalogue of the Grace K. Babson
Collection of the Works of Isaac Newton*, with an account of
the great manuscripts acquired from the Portsmouth sale.
Here were full descriptions of alchemical MSS, Newton's treatise in MS on Solomon's Temple, notes on the Athanasian
creed, and other theological documents. But there was no
further new revelation from the MSS until Hall's second paper,
in 1955, on "Further Optical Experiments of Newton." My
own *Franklin and Newton* of 1956 did not draw on MSS at
all, since its aim was to trace the public tradition of Newtonian

science during the 18th century.[113] In 1953, however, Professor Turnbull revealed some aspects of Newton's calculations of lunar gravity of 1665–66, but he did so not in a scholarly journal but in the *Manchester Guardian*.[114]

I find that the next use of MSS, in 1957, was again by Rupert Hall, on Newton's early calculation of central forces. And in the following year, 1958, there was the first of a series of papers by A. Rupert Hall and Marie Boas Hall, drawing on Newton's MSS — this one on Newton's chemical experiments. It was in this same year that I brought out my edition of Newton's published *Papers & Letters on Natural Philosophy*.

In 1959, the first volume of the long-awaited edition of Newton's correspondence heralded a new wealth of available source materials for understanding the life and thought of Isaac Newton, and in 1962, A.R. Hall and Marie Boas Hall continued the pioneer work of the third revelation of Newton with their volume of *Unpublished Scientific Papers of Isaac Newton*. The Halls listed the major scholars known to them who had used or quoted from Newton's manuscripts. Among the names in their list were D. Geoghegan, who in 1957 had published a few extracts from "the alchemical papers in King's College;" F. Sherwood Taylor, who in that same year printed "a composite of quotations from alchemical authors put together by Newton;" and Sir John Craig, who had used "the papers sold in 1936, though printing none *in extenso*."[115] The Halls also referred to David Eugene Smith, who in 1927 had published two documents; Alexandre Koyré, who in 1961 had published the MS texts of Newton's "Rules"; J.W. Herivel, who in 1960 and 1961 had published his first extracts from Newton's early studies of dynamics; and R.S. Westfall, who in 1958 had discussed "Newton's theology with some reference to the King's College papers." It was not a very impressive list, and it gave no hint of the "Newton industry" just coming into being.

I shall not attempt to summarize the contents of the Halls' seminal volume. But there are at least four extraordinary revelations about Newton in it. One is an essay which the Halls entitled "De gravitatione et aequipondio fluidorum," a general discussion of the principles of physics based upon young Newton's reading in Descartes' *Principles of Philosophy* and published scientific correspondence. Here was an indication of the profound influence of Descartes' science and philosophy upon Newton. Another was the revelation of Newton's intended but incomplete "Conclusio" written for his *Principles*, in which Newton expressed his aim of producing a science of particulate matter equivalent to his science of gross bodies. A third was the analysis of the stages of composition of the "General Scholium" with its mysterious reference to "subtle spirit," which turned out to be Hauksbee's electrical effluvia. Finally, the Halls showed how Newton was tending toward a philosophy of nature in which he added the concept of particulate forces (attraction and repulsion) to the received categories or principles of the "mechanical philosophy" — matter and motion.

5. WHAT HAS BEEN REVEALED

I shall not attempt here to make a complete review of all of the new revelations brought about by the study of the manuscripts. To do so would be tantamount to making a critical inventory of the whole corpus of Newton scholarship during the last 20 years or so. But I shall indicate some of the highlights of the scholarly work that constitutes the third and final revelation.[116] To me, one of the most interesting parts of the revelation has been the demonstration of the true importance of Descartes in the development of Newton's scientific and mathematical thought. It is generally known that in his *Principles* Newton refers to Descartes only indirectly, in a proof at the end of Book Two that the system of vortices is inconsistent with the astronomical phenomena, namely, Kepler's laws of planetary motion.[117] Mathematicians and historians, going back at least to Clairaut and Lagrange,[118] have even suggested that the whole purpose of Book Two was to demolish the Cartesian theory of vortices. Not only was Newton's dynamical astronomy thus supposed to be a frontal attack on the Cartesian scientific system, but this was the case also in mathematics. Newton's relation to Descartes was charaterized by the remarks quoted by Brewster that Newton's copy of Descartes' *Geometry* bore the comments in Newton's hand, again and again, "Error" or "non est Geom."[119] Accordingly, it came as a considerable surprise — as first shown, with full documentary detail, by Rupert and Marie Hall[120] that Newton had made a careful study of Descartes' writings and that many of his own scientific ideas — for instance, those about dynamics and inertia — were developed as he contemplated the writings of Descartes. The relation between Descartes' physical concepts and Newton's was clarified by the writings of Alexandre Koyré, who traced the relationship between Newton's definition and statement of the law of inertia and Descartes' statement,[121] a study which I myself helped to complete by showing the steps of transmission and transformation by which Newton attained his own first law of motion from Descartes' law of nature.[122] It even turns out that the title of Newton's "Mathematical Principles of Natural Philosophy" is only a transformation of Descartes' title "Principles of Philosophy." The very phrase used by Newton, "Axiomata, sive Leges Motus,"[123] was a transformation of what he found in Descartes' *Principles*, "Regulae quaedem sive leges naturae."[124] Not only did Newton write in terms of the new idea of a "state" of motion (which, as Koyré showed, was obtained directly from Descartes),[125] but I found that even such a phrase as "quantum in se est" which Newton used for inertia was taken directly from Descartes in this context; it came originally from Lucretius. Thus I found a dramatic illustration of how Newton's concepts were born by transformation of Descartes' ideas.[126] At the same time, Whiteside showed in the first volume of his monumental edition of *The Mathematical Papers of Isaac Newton* that Newton's fundamental ideas of the calculus were first forged and developed in his study of Descartes' *Geometry*, in a Latin edition by Schooten with tracts by other mathematicians. Thus there could no longer be any doubt whatever of the supreme importance of Descartes for Newton's dynamics and eventually celestial mechanics, as well as his invention of the calculus. And, as it finally turned out, the volume of Descartes'

Geometry in which Newton had written "Error, Error" did not contain this word as a characterization of Cartesian mathematics as a whole, but indicated where Descartes had made errors; and "non est Geom." appeared in certain places where Newton indicated that the discussion by Descartes was not from a narrow and strict point of view to be considered "geometry."[127]

Another aspect of Newton's thought revealed by the manuscripts has been studied primarily by Henry Guerlac,[128] who has traced the vagaries or variations in Newton's concept of the aether and the degree of his adherence to a belief in the aether. Thus, while Newton early believed in an aether that had a kind of substance, he then went through a period in which he thought that the aether — if it existed at all — had to be so tenuous that it could not produce most of the effects that he wished to attribute to it. Then later on he became excited by the work of Hauksbee and adopted a different kind of aether or "aetherial medium" in the final queries of the *Opticks*.[129] R.S. Westfall has traced the relations between Newton's changing views about the aether and his concept of force.[130] Meanwhile, J.E. McGuire, working alone and also with P.M. Rattansi, showed how Newton believed in a priscan wisdom and thus thought that the scientific knowledge attained by Newton himself had largely been known to ancient seers or sages in Greece or Asia Minor.[131] Newton considered that many of the great advances in science in his day (including his own discovery of universal gravity) were to a large degree only rediscoveries of what had been known long before. McGuire has also used the manuscripts to show the development of Newton's ideas about transmutation and transformation of matter and has elucidated Newton's conception of "passive" and "active" forces in matter.[132] This has been a very valuable part of our understanding of Newton's concept of force in general and of the properties of matter, which are of course basic to his physics. At the same time, Frank Manuel has made a very fundamental contribution to our understanding of Newton's historical studies, notably his chronologies, and the stages of development of his religious ideas.[133] He has also drawn heavily on the corpus of Newtonian MSS for his *Portrait of Isaac Newton* (1968). The Halls and R.S. Westfall have written about Newton's ideas concerning matter and force. In particular, Westfall has used the manuscripts of Newton not only to trace the development of Newton's idea of force, but to elucidate what he calls Newton's radical revision of the "mechanical philosophy" of Descartes to which he generally adhered, according to which all phenomena were to be explained by matter and motion.[134] Westfall sees Newton as having added to that received philosophy the concept of force.[135] Westfall has also studied the optical manuscripts of Newton, another aspect of tracing the development of Newton's ideas concerning the aether.[136] It should be added that J.A. Lohne and Alan Shapiro have also worked fruitfully with the optical manuscripts.[137] Among other interesting revelations here is the fact that Newton's great paper on the nature of light and colors (1672) turns out to be something of a "scenario," because the way in which he describes the events of his exploration of dispersion and his description of his own reaction to his observations of prismatic spectra cannot be squared with the evidence of his prior knowledge as provided by the manuscript notebooks.[138] It should be noted that Zev Bechler has made an interesting set of studies of Newton's attempts to formulate a mathematical model for optical theory, in a style somewhat like that adopted for dynamics and celestial mechanics in Newton's *Principles*.[139] Westfall has also made a thorough study of Newton's early theological manuscripts and has shown among other things that Newton's concern for theology arose when it became necessary for him to contemplate holy orders in order to keep his Trinity College Fellowship. In this, Westfall has drawn heavily on the Yahuda manuscripts, now in the University of Jerusalem and acquired by A.S. Yahuda from the Portsmouth sale at Sotheby's.[140] This subject has also been explored in an illuminating manner by Frank Manuel in his volume on Newton's religion, based upon this same collection of Newtonian manuscripts in Jerusalem.[141]

One of the long-standing puzzles about Newton's scientific work was how he could have claimed to have used the law for centrifugal force (v^2/r) in the 1660's in order to derive the inverse-square law of force for uniform circular motion.[142] The problem was one of dates, since Huygens did not publish the law until 1673 in his *Horologium oscillatorium*. The MSS contain the answer, as J.W. Herivel discovered.[143] He found that Newton had come upon this law independently about a decade or so before the publication of Huygens's book. Newton's derivation and the form in which he presented the law differ greatly from what is found in Huygens's book (which contains no derivatives or proof, but only a bare statement of the law in words). Since Newton is apt to be not wholly trustworthy on questions of dates and discoveries, it is pleasant to be able to record that in this case the MSS show that he had discovered this law just as he said he had done.

There is one further aspect of this third revelation which I have reserved until last, because it is in many ways the most striking and the most controversial. I refer here to Newton and hermeticism in general, and Newton's relation to alchemy in particular.

Today we look on Newton's alchemy in a way that is totally different from that of the 19th-century commentators on Newton, of whom Brewster is a striking example. Part of the third revelation concerning Newton has been the result of carefully reading his papers on alchemy and finding that during the most creative period of his life Newton was a serious student of alchemy, as in fact Brewster reluctantly had to admit. But we do not necessarily approach the subject today by considering it contemptible. After all, modern atomic and nuclear physics has shown that Newton was distressingly right when he said that Nature delights in transmutations.[144] We have learned in our own century that transmutations of the elements are constantly going on naturally all around us as one atom dies and gives birth to another in all the radioactive elements and that these transformations have been going on since the beginning of matter.

In this area we are indebted to F. Sherwood Taylor and D. Geoghegan[145] for brave beginnings and to A. Rupert and Marie Boas Hall[146] for serious inquiries, carried on by

Richard S. Westfall.[147] But of greatest consequence are two full-length works of major importance on Newton's alchemical manuscripts and their meaning by Betty Jo Teeter Dobbs[148] and by Karin Figala. As a result of these studies, it is now, as the lawyers say, "open and notorious" that Newton was so deeply steeped in his alchemical studies and researches that — to use a kind of alchemical term — much of his scientific thinking must obviously have been "tinctured" with alchemical ideas, imagery, and theories.[149] For example, Newton's concept of the aether was clearly related to his alchemical thinking.[150] And there can be, it seems to me, no doubt whatsoever (a conclusion which is so obvious that it would seem almost supererogatory to say it, save that no one did say it until fairly recently) that Newton's extensive reflections on the "theory of matter," and especially on the composition of matter and the particulate forces in matter, must be closely related to and possibly even to some degree derived from the realm of alchemy.

And so the study and the editing of Newton's manuscripts show that Keynes was to a degree correct. There is revealed to us a man who, during the three decades of his residence in Cambridge, most of it as Lucasian Professor of Mathematics, was devoting intense creative energies to studying the literature of alchemy — both esoteric and exoteric — and making alchemical experiments, working out the meaning of the prophetic books of the Bible (Daniel and Revelation), trying to find the wisdom of ancient sages and seers, solving (to his own satisfaction) problems of biblical and historical chronology, studying church history, and wrestling with problems of pure theology. Is this the same Newton who is revered as the founder of modern rational science? In the extreme it has been suggested that we have "perhaps mistaken the thrust of Newton's career," that whereas "to us, the *Principia* inevitably appears as [the] ... climax [of that career], in Newton's perspective it may have seemed more like an interruption of his primary labor."[151]

Betty Jo Teeter Dobbs, who has produced exemplary studies of the principles and practices of alchemy as revealed in Newton's MSS, comes to the general conclusion that it was "the *wedding* of the Hermetic tradition with the mechanical philosophy which produced modern science as its offspring." Part of the reason is that "Newton's concept of forces between particles derived initially from terrestrial phenomena, especially chemical ones," and that "it was the concept of gravitation, that fundamental tenet of Newton's law of universal gravitation, which was so derived." She would thus suggest that "the 'active Principles' of the Hermetic tradition" were "incorporated into the attractive force of gravity."[152]

I believe we must be extremely careful about this third revelation, for there is a temptation to assume that because Newton had such deep interests in alchemy and prophecy and ancient wisdom he produced his positive science out of these elements. But I believe the documents do not support this position. Newton, it seems to me, was not unusual because of his concern with prophecy, alchemy, and ancient wisdom. Indeed, when we think of the similar interests of Boyle and Locke, we find that it would have been unusual if Newton had *not* been so concerned.[153] To me, it is not significant that the founder of our rational mathematics and physical science should have been so steeped in esoteric subjects, but that he could have under those conditions, or in spite of those conditions, produced his masterpiece of modern hard science and established or inaugurated the first clearly recognized revolution in modern physical science. But, as Frances Yates wisely remarked to me when I discussed this extraordinary aspect of Newton's career with her, "We must remember that Newton was a genius."[153 a]

6. THE DOCUMENTS OF THE THIRD REVELATION

Let me now turn to the documents that have enabled us to make this third revelation. The mass of documentary materials that comprise the corpus of Newtonian MSS is staggering in its extent. A literal pack rat, he saved scraps of paper from his college days and his early notebooks as a student. There remain thousands of MS pages relating to optics, astronomy, mechanics, mathematics, chronology, theology, alchemy, and the Mint, and a huge stack devoted to the controversy with Leibniz on priority in the matter of the calculus. There are books from his library with extensive MS annotations. The result is that we can trace the development of Newton's ideas in agonizing detail in many domains of his intellectual interest. But there is one major exception. We do not have the working papers in which he made the rough drafts and notes for the *Mathematical Principles of Natural Philosophy*. There are contemporaneous stories about Newton having burned some of his papers, and perhaps these were among the ones thrown into the flames. We can trace the alterations — proposed and actual — to the *Principles* once it was cast in all but final form, but we do not know how he discovered and proved his theorems.[154] I myself am convinced that the path of Newton's intellectual invention proceeded more or less in the order and form in which he presented his results in the *Principles*. Newton, however, alleged that the theorems in large part had been "invented by [the method of] Analysis." But, as he said, "considering that the Ancients ... admitted nothing into Geometry before it was demonstrated by Composition [or Synthesis], I composed what I invented by Analysis to make it more Geometrically authentic & fit for the publick."[155] This was part of Newton's campaign to make it appear that he had actually used the newly invented calculus in the first stages of the *Principles* and then rewritten his work "in words at length after the manner of the Ancients without Analytical calculations." Such was his answer to the charge raised by the Leibnizians: If he really had invented the fluxional calculus, how could he possibly have written the *Principles* without using fluxions? Could it be that he destroyed this particular set of papers so as to be able to defend an invented scenario of discovery without having material evidence at hand to disturb his conscience?[156]

When the first edition of the *Principles* was published in 1687, Newton prepared at least two special copies to record emendations for a future edition — one was interleaved and specially bound for this purpose. And he did the same for the

second edition in preparation for an eventual third edition.[157]
I know of no author at this time who made such specially
annotated and interleaved copies of his works. And so when
Alexandre Koyré, Anne Whitman, and I came to edit the
Principles, we were able to collate the three printed versions,
the printer's MS, an annotated and an interleaved first edition,
and an annotated and an interleaved second edition — eight
in all.

Some of the differences are minor, some of great significance. In the first edition, "The System of the Universe"
(Book 3) opens with a set of hypotheses. In the second edition,
some of them become phenomena.[157a] While writing out the
concluding General Scholium for the second edition (1713),
with its famous slogan *Hypotheses non fingo* ("I frame [or
feign] no hypotheses"), Newton said that whatever is neither a
phenomenon nor deduced from phenomena is a hypothesis.
This statement occurs plainly in the published version. Had
he changed his mind? In any event, there are still three
plainly labeled hypotheses in the final *Principles*, despite
Hypotheses non fingo.[157b]

Of the major changes in successive editions, attention may
be called to the following. In Book One of the *Principles*, in
the first edition, prop. 16 proves the falsity of the rule of
planetary motions in which it is supposed that the orbital
speed in an ellipse is inversely proportional to the planet's
distance from the sun. This result is of more than ordinary interest, since Hooke had asserted in a letter to Newton (6 January 1680) that if the solar force varies inversely as the square
of the distance, the speed will be "as Kepler Supposes Recip-
rocall to the Distance."[158] Hooke evidently was not aware
that this speed law had been rejected by Kepler and is in fact
inconsistent with an inverse-square law of force. Hooke cited
this letter to bolster his claim that he had anticipated Newton
in the matter of the inverse-square law of force, and Newton
replied by sending on to Halley a new scholium for prop. 4,
giving a youthful demonstration of the law of centrifugal/
centripetal force for uniform circular motion, which leads by
the simplest algebra to the inverse-square law. For the second

edition of the *Principles*, Newton shifted to prop.2 the corollaries originally following prop.1 of Book One, and he inserted a new set of corollaries following prop.1. The first of these contains the statement of the true law of speed (that it is proportional, not inversely to the distance from the sun to the planet's position, but to the perpendicular distance from the sun to the tangent drawn through that position). Newton's effective reply to Hooke was thus advanced from prop. 16 to the extremely prominent place of the first corollary to the first proposition in the first book of the *Principles*.[159]

Another important change was to correct the proof of prop. 10 of Book Two. A significant error in the proof had been brought to Newton's attention by Nikolaus Bernoulli after the pages containing this proof had been printed off for the second edition. For the new proof it was thus necessary to reprint the whole sheet of signature "Hh" and the leaf containing pages 233–34, which is a cancel pasted onto the stub of the original leaf in every copy of the *Principles* with which I am familiar.[160] In the second edition, most of Section 7 of Book Two, on the resistance of fluids and on the motion of a fluid flowing out of a vessel, was completely recast.[161] As mentioned above, there were significant alterations in the opening of Book Three, the original "Hypotheses" being converted largely into "Phaenomena" and "Regulae Philosophandi." And Newton also completely rewrote and expanded the scholium following prop. 35 of Book Three, in which he claimed to have derived the theory of the moon's motion entirely from mathematical considerations of the action of gravitational forces of the sun and the earth on the moon.[162]

The title pages of each of Newton's major treatises offer puzzles to the prospective editor. For example, there exist two different forms of the title page of the *Principles* in the first edition (1687). One bears the name of the printer Joseph Streater and says: "Prostat apud plures Bibliopolas." The other (sometimes called "a reissue of the first edition") differs only in that the imprint declares: "Prostant Venales apud *Sam. Smith* ad insignia Principis *Walliae* in Coemiterio D. *Pauli*, aliosq; nonnullos Bibliopolas." It has been conjectured that the copies without "*Sam. Smith*" in the imprint may have been intended for sale abroad and those with "*Sam. Smith*" for home consumption.[163] What is perhaps of even greater interest is the fact that Samuel Pepys's name appears more prominently than Newton's. In Newton's annotated copy of the first edition, the name of the learned diarist has been cancelled and the form of Newton's name has been revised and his rank and position (*Sir* Isaac Newton, President of the Royal Society) have been brought up to date — by Richard Bentley.[163a]

The title page of the *Opticks* (1704) is even more puzzling, for it does not contain the name of the author. This was hardly an oversight, but rather intentional, since there exists at least one special copy ("of record"?) in which the lines of type of the title page have been slightly rearranged to accommodate the additional line, placed between two rules, "By ISAAC NEWTON."[164] We do not know why Newton did not want his name on the title page (the preface is signed "I.N."), but there are two possible reasons for this action. The first is that the *Opticks* is written in the vernacular. We may recall that Christiaan Huygens's *Traité de la lumière* (also written in the vernacular) was similarly published without the author's name on the title page, which bears only the initials, "Par C.H.D.Z." But there exist at least two copies in which — as with the one example of Newton's *Opticks* — the author's name is given in full: "Par Monsieur **Christian Huygens**, Seigneur de Zeelhem."[164a] Newton's *Opticks* was written up in words, with quantitative results of experiments and some calculations, but not with proofs of propositions by mathematical methods (i.e., geometry, algebra or ratios, fluxions, infinite series, etc) from first principles. The propositions tend to have a "Proof by Experiments." The reason is not that Newton did not want to develop physical optics mathematically in what I have called "the Newtonian style." Rather, his attempts to do so in terms of various proposed mathematico-physical models proved to be failures. In this sense, the form of the *Opticks* was a kind of confession of failure, suggesting it to be an imperfect work suitable only for publication in a vernacular language and presumably not fully worthy of bearing the author's name.[164b]

At the height of the controversy with Leibniz, the Royal Society — at Leibniz's request — mounted an investigation. They appointed a so-called international committee which produced their famous report, the *Commercium epistolicum*, in which it is claimed that Newton was the sole and primary inventor of the calculus.[165] Leibniz was judged to have been a plagiarist. Looking at the composition of the committee, no one ever could have supposed it impartial. But what we now know from the study of Newton's MSS is that Newton actually drafted the report, for there exist a large number of drafts and versions of the report written out in his own hand.[166] We can watch Newton ask himself whether he would have the committee say, "We are satisfied that Mr. Newton invented the method of fluxions before 1669," or whether it might sound more convincing to say simply, "We find that he invented the method of fluxions before 1669." Perhaps it would be even better to put it, "We are satisfied that Mr. Newton was the first author of the method." He liked that, but decided it was not strong enough, so he added some evidence to back it up and concluded, "... for which reason we reckon Mr. Newton the first inventor." When the anonymous *Commercium* was eventually published, there appeared a lengthy book review of it in the *Philosophical Transactions of the Royal Society of London*. It was long suspected that Newton must have helped write this review, but the MSS show dozens of versions of it in his own hand. He was the sole author. Finally, when the *Commercium* was reprinted in 1722 in a second edition, this review was added as an introduction, still anonymous, but translated into Latin. But now there was added a new anonymous preface commending the review and emphasizing its major points. Who wrote it? Isaac Newton — as is shown by the many MS versions of it in his own hand.[166a]

Since I have mentioned the number of different versions of the same text in Newton's MSS, it is appropriate to call attention to one of the major problems in editing Newton's unpublished writings. Not only are there successive versions or drafts, but Newton had the maddening habit of making multiple copies of the same document, sometimes with only minor variations. He even copied out whole sections of books from his own library. I have referred (in section 2 *supra*) to Brewster's astonishment on finding that Newton had copied out texts (in part or in full) of alchemical treatises, some of them appearing twice in identical versions. A theological MS in the Keynes Collection called "Irenicum, or Ecclesiastical Polity Tending to Peace" exists in seven almost identical autograph drafts. Whiston recorded that Newton wrote out "eighteen copies of the first and principal chapter of the Chronology with his own hand but little different from one another." The small tract *De motu corporum*, preliminary to the *Principles*, exists (as I have mentioned earlier) in at least five (and possibly six) variant versions with different titles.[167] There are four separate commentaries on Daniel and the Apocalypse. The only saving grace for an editor is that Newton's handwriting is generally clear and easy to read. It has even been conjectured that Newton may have delighted in copying out extracts from printed works as well as his own compositions because he was overly enamored of his own handwriting. Here is yet another textual mystery.

There is no plan or program for producing a uniform series of all of Newton's writings. A somewhat similar format has been adopted by Cambridge University Press for the seven-volume set of Newton's *Correspondence*, the eight volumes of D.T. Whiteside's edition of *The Mathematical Papers of Isaac Newton*, and the three volumes of our edition of Newton's *Philosophiae naturalis principia mathematica* with variant readings. But the same publisher used a different format for the Halls' *Unpublished Scientific Papers of Isaac Newton*, and it is doubtful whether the grand style and format can withstand the pressures of inflation.

Whoever laments the lack of a great edition of all of Newton's writings should be aware of the paradox that there is not a one-to-one correspondence between the existence of a great scholarly edition of a scientist's works and a body of significant scholarly writings concerning that figure. A notable example is Christiaan Huygens, one of the major mathematicians and scientists of the second half of the 17th century — easily the greatest scientist of his time but for Newton. In fact, Huygens is the only scientist of Newton's day to whom Newton applied the appellation *summus*. The edition of Huygens's writings is a tremendous monument to scholarship, unrivalled in the annals of science. Published by the Dutch Society of Sciences, the edition eventually filled 22 magnificent volumes, the first appearing in 1888 and the last in 1950. Words cannot convey the quality of this edition. The volumes are in a large quarto size, beautifully printed in large type. The paper is of an extravagant quality, handmade specially for this edition and watermarked "Christiaan Huygens." Each subject and each major paper is introduced by a historical essay, and there are extensive scholarly annotations. Furthermore, each volume has three long and complete indexes: one of books and articles mentioned in the text or in the notes and introductions, another of persons mentioned, and a third of subjects. It is an edition that puts to shame all others. And yet it must be reported that the last quarter century has produced very little in the way of scholarly articles on Huygens and his work. There are no major studies of importance on his contributions to astronomy (his telescopes, his resolution of Saturn's ring, his discovery of a satellite of Saturn), nor of his work in geometry and analysis (including his work on the cycloid), his discovery of the laws of impact, his great study of circular motion and his finding of the laws of "centrifugal" force, nor is there even an adequate critical and scholarly analysis of his discovery of the isochronism of the epicycloidal pendulum and the invention of the clock escapement. There is not even a true biography of Huygens worthy of the man and on a par with the great edition of his *Oeuvres*.

By contrast, the Newton industry — like the Darwin industry — goes on apace. One can scarcely keep up with all the books and articles in these fields. In both cases, radical new interpretations have been emerging — based on extensive use of the manuscripts. Yet in the case of both Newton and

Darwin there is no real edition of their works, although an edition of Darwin's correspondence is in progress.

Will there be a fourth revelation of Isaac Newton, or have we reached the final stages of knowledge with the completion of the trinity? I very much doubt that there will be a new revelation as far-reaching and as profound as the third has been. But in this regard historians would be wise to follow the advice given to young chemists by Harvard's Professor E.P. Kohler. A lecture-demonstration had ended in an explosion that destroyed the lecture table and the front of the lecture room, instead of merely producing the change in color and substance that he had announced to his class in organic chemistry. In these matters, he said, a chemist should be a historian and not a prophet.

NOTES

1. The original publications of Isaac Newton are listed in Babson (1950), Gray (1907), and Wallis (1977); the work by Wallis contains also references to the secondary literature. A good guide to the main scholarly works concerning Newton is to be found in Cohen (1974). The current literature is listed in the annual Critical Bibliography published in *Isis*, the official quarterly journal of the History of Science Society. The advance of Newton scholarship can be followed year by year during a half-century in Pighetti (1960).
2. On the circulation and printing of this paper in Newton's day, see the introduction to the facsimile reprint of it in Newton (1958). An admirable discussion of the publication of Newton's writings is to be found in the introduction to the first volume of D.T. Whiteside's edition of Newton's *Mathematical papers*.
3. These appear at the beginning of the volume. See Cohen (1971). An edition of Newton's *Principles*, with variant readings, was published in 1972. A new English translation by Anne Whitman and the writer is currently being completed for publication.
4. The *Opticks* is available in a paperback reprint (1952). A scholarly edition of this work, with an analysis of the difference between the several editions, has been completed for publication by Henry Guerlac.

5. Of course, Newton's publications on chronology and the interpretation of the prophetic books of Scripture were available to all, and there were hints aplenty concerning Newton's interest in alchemy. A major text of Newton's, giving a clue to the fact that Newton's interests were not limited to mathematical physics and experiment, was published by Gregory in 1832.

6. Of course, during the 18th century the Cartesians and various other groups did not accept the Newtonian principles and so did not look upon Newton as the lawgiver. For representations of Newton in art, see the article by Haskell in Palter (1970); also Cohen (1979).

7. See Buchdahl (1961).

8. Malone (1948), 101.

9. See Westfall (1980), Manuel (1959, 1963, 1974).

10. See Dobbs (1975), Figala (1977, 1977a).

11. See McGuire & Rattansi (1966).

12. See Munby (1952b).

13. The fullest account of the history of Newton's manuscripts is to be found in D.T. Whiteside's introduction to the first volume of his edition of Newton's *Mathematical papers*.

14. E.g., Mach (1960), 236-7.

15. See Cohen (1971), ch 9, section 7.

16. *Ibid*, 242.

17. See Koyré (1960); the changes in the queries are indicated in Horsley's edition (1779-85). See Guerlac's edition (referred to in note 4 *supra*).

18. Koyré & Cohen (1961, 1962); see in Priestley (1970).

19. This is discussed in Cohen (1969).

20. In a letter to Bentley (10 Dec. 1692), Newton said: "When I wrote my treatise about our Systeme I had an eye upon such Principles as might work wth considering men for the beleife of a Deity & nothing can rejoyce me more then to find it usefull for that purpose." See *Correspondence, 3*, 233.

21. The translation "I feign" for "fingo" was suggested by Alexandre Koyré; see Cohen (1962). See query 31 in the second and later English editions.

22. The discussions of these questions occur in the second part of the last paragraph of the concluding query 31 in the second and later editions.

23. This occurs in query 30: "Nature ... seems delighted with Transmutations."

24. See the edition of Newton's *Principles* (1972) with variant readings, p 87 (line 9), p 89 (lines 1, 3, 6, 7, 12, 16, 29), p 90 (line 32), p 402 (line 20).

25. See Cohen (1966), Koyré (1965).

26. This hypothesis was eliminated in the second edition.

27. See Cohen (1966), and especially McGuire (1967).
28. On the way in which it was used, see Cohen (1966). See also McMullin (1978).
29. I have indicated, in Cohen (1966), that this was a hypothesis of the Aristotelians and Cartesians, rather than Newton's own belief.
30. Cohen (1964).
31. *Ibid.*
32. See Manuel (1963).
33. *Ibid.*
34. *Ibid.*
35. See Westfall (1980).
36. See Manuel (1974).
37. A catalogue of Napier's works by W.R. MacDonald is given in the latter's English translation of Napier's *Canon* (1889).
38. Manuel (1974), 99.
39. *Ibid*, 99-100. See Hill (1965).
40. Cf, e.g., Hill (1965), 7.
41. Manuel (1974), 90-1.
42. *Ibid*, 92.
43. For an account of Newton's method, see Manuel (1963, 1974).
44. Manuel (1974), 93.
45. Quoting from McLachlan (1950), 119.
46. See Cohen (1960), 500-1.
47. Newton (1733).
48. Quoted from D.T. Whiteside (1967), introduction to *Math. papers, 1*, xviii.
49. *Ibid*, xix.
50. *Ibid*, xix-xx.
51. *Ibid*, xx, n 12.
52. Brewster (1855), *2*, 342-6.
53. McLachlan published only a selection, in which the texts were chosen to illustrate a particular point of view. It would be a great desideratum to bring out a rather fuller selection of Newton's theological writings, including texts from the Yahuda MSS now in Jerusalem.
54. Manuel (1963); also see Manuel (1974).
55. *Op cit*, xx, n 15.
56. These are now largely to be found in the Keynes MSS in the library of King's College in Cambridge.
57. For an account of Conduitt's activities in relation to these Newtonian documents, see Whiteside, *op cit*.
58. See DeMorgan (1885).
59. Whiteside, *op cit* xxii-xxiii.

60. *Ibid.*
61. See the complete catalogue, Portsmouth Collection (1888).
62. Newton (1779-85).
63. See Whiteside, *op cit.*, xxvii.
64. This tract was published by Rigaud (1838), app 1, 1-19, from the text in the Royal Society. Versions based on the MSS in the University Library, Cambridge, have been published in Ball (1893), 51-6; Hall & Hall (1962), 243-67; Herivel (1965), 257-74; and Whiteside (*Math. papers, 6*, 30-80). On the background to the composition of *De motu*, see Cohen (1970), ch 3, 47-81 (esp 54-62); on its significance, see Cohen (1980), ch 5 (esp sections 5.5, 5.6).
65. There are two states of the first edition, one having Edinburgh and London on the title page, the other Edinburgh and Boston, both 1855; the second edition (1860) has only Edinburgh. A facsimile reprint (1965) of the first edition includes an introduction by R.S. Westfall.
66. More (1934), vi.
67. Introduction (1967) to *Math. papers, 1*, xxix.
68. Brewster (1855), *1*, vii-viii, x.
69. *Ibid*, x.
70. See Stukeley (1936), *passim*.
71. *Ibid*, 20; see Cohen (1946).
72. See McKie & DeBeer (1952).
73. Actually, Stukeley's example can serve as a "cautionary tale" to all practicing historians of science. In fact, it was on contemplating Stukeley's example that I began a program of oral history in relation to certain crucial developments in the history of contemporary physics and in the rise of the computer.
74. Brewster (1855), *2*, 371-6.
75. *Ibid*, 372.
76. *Ibid*.
77. *Ibid*, 372-3.
78. *Ibid*, 374.
79. *Ibid*.
80. *Ibid*, 374-6.
81. *Ibid*, 371-2.
82. *Ibid*, 372, n 1.
83. See note 65 *supra*.
84. These occur primarily in vol 2, ch 24; also in appendixes 29-30.
85. Letter from Lord Portsmouth to the Vice Chancellor of Cambridge University, 23 July 1872; quoted in Whiteside's "General Introduction" to vol 1 of his edition of Newton's *Math. papers*, p xxxi.
86. From a note by Lord Portsmouth, 2 Aug. 1872 (ULC MS Add 2588, ff 494-5), quoted by Whiteside, *op cit*, xxxi.

87. *Ibid*, f 496

87a *Ibid*; also, preface to Portsmouth Collection (1888), ix.

88. Portsmouth Collection (1888).

89. The collection is not officially known as "The Portsmouth Collection," and it is catalogued as a series of separate or individual entries, one for each group of manuscripts or each book. Since the catalogue (1888) is officially entitled *A catalogue of the Portsmouth Collection of small books and papers* ..., the portion given to the University Library is generally (but only informally) known as the Portsmouth Collection.

90. Portsmouth Collection (1888), ix-x.

91. The catalogue as printed would give the user no idea that the papers relating to the questions of priority in the invention of the calculus (ULC MS Add 3968) occupy some thousand manuscript pages. For a report on these, with critical comments and extracts, see vol 8 of D.T. Whiteside's edition of Newton's *Math. papers*; also, Hall (1980).

92. The three appendixes deal with "The form of the Solid of Least Resistance" (see schol. to prop. 35 of book 2 of Newton's *Principles*), "A List of Propositions in the Lunar Theory intended to be inserted in a second edition of the *Principia*," and "The motion of the Apogee in an elliptic orbit of very small eccentricity, caused by given disturbing forces." Often reprinted and quoted is an autobiographical statement of Newton's about the stages of his discovery of his main ideas on celestial dynamics (p xviii); a complete version of this document, with critical comments, has been published in Cohen (1971), supp 1.

93. These are largely collected together in ULC MS Add. 4007.

94. *Op cit*, xxxiii.

95. This is reprinted, together with other essays, in Ball (1918).

96. Ball (1893).

97. *Op cit*, xxxiv.

98. Fraser's publications are listed in Wallis & Wallis (1977). See especially, Fraser (1927).

99. Witting (1911-12); see Whiteside, *op cit*, xxxiv.

00. More (1934), 158.

01. *Ibid*, 159.

02. *Ibid*, 159, n 6.

03. *Ibid*, 641.

04. *Ibid*, 644.

05. *Ibid*.

05a In the preface to his biography (p vi), More castigated Brewster for having adopted "the rôle of advocate to 'The High Priest of Science' as he calls Newton" and for portraying his hero "without blemish intellectually and morally." More noted that Brewster had said that "where he found evidence which confirmed facts known to reflect adversely on Newton's character, he published it; but if the facts were not previously known, he felt bound in honour to respect the privacy of his discovery." But in the end More himself admitted (p vii): "There is absolutely nothing in his life so serious that it should have been suppressed." I have always found this a curious statement, since it seems to imply that if there had been something "serious" in Newton's life, then "it should have been suppressed." And it is to be noted that although More thought that Brewster had gone to extremes in defending his hero, the critical reader today cannot help but observe how More did the same. More (p 333) found it necessary to attack "Professor Einstein's Generalised Theory of Relativity" for apparently daring to diminish the greatness or permanence of the system of dynamics of Newton's *Principles*. He would have Einstein's work be "merely a logical exercise of the active mind," which "ignores the world of brute facts." It "may be interesting, but it ultimately evaporates into a scholasticism. And if it persists, it will cause the decadence of science as surely as the mediaeval scholasticism preceded the decadence of religion." So much, then, for the popular belief that "modern criticism has at last broken down the classical mechanics."

Indeed, More felt the need of defending not only Newton against the onslaught of the physics of the 20th century, but also Aristotle. He said (p 332): "It is a notable fact that these two works [Newton's *Principles* and Aristotle's *Organon*], probably the two most stupendous creations of the scientific brain, are now under attack — the *Organon* by modern symbolists in logic, and the *Principia* by the relativists in physics." It was More's judgement that "Aristotle and Newton will be honoured and *used* when the modernists are long forgotten."

106. Munby (1952); see Sotheby (1936).
107. See Munby (1952).
108. See Harrison (1978).
109. See Royal Society (1947).
110. This new version, prepared by Anne Whitman and me, will be published by Harvard University Press and Cambridge University Press.
110a Others, whose work is referred to below, who have contributed to this third revelation are Zev Bechler, Joan L. Hawes, and Peter Heimann. See also the important researches on Newton's prism experiments and telescope by A.A. Mills.
111. Keynes's essay was published in Royal Society (1947) and has been since reprinted with other essays of his.
112. Hall (1948).

13. Indeed, despite some obvious faults and its limitations, the presentation of Newton in this volume has a special value today, since it indicates the "public" or "semi-public" view of Newton available in the two centuries following Newton's death before our attention was riveted to some of the more startling aspects of Newton's private life, which have been brought to light by recent studies of his manuscripts.

14. Turnbull (1953).

15. See Craig (1946), *Newton at the Mint*. An interesting use of the Mint MSS has been made by Manuel in ch 11 of his *Portrait* (1968).

16. The limitations of space prevent my giving here even an approximation to what could be considered *all* of the major revelations brought about by the study of the Newtonian MSS. Accordingly, the examples that follow should not be considered as constituting in any sense a definitive set of what I consider to be the first-rate works of Newtonian scholarship of the last three decades or so. In other words, the omission of the name of any particular scholar should certainly *not* be taken to imply that I do not esteem his or her work as highly as those that I mention or discuss. In fact, some of the particular choices and omissions have resulted from an attempt to give an indication of the different kinds of scholarship, rather than to make a selection of the highest forms of scholarship to be recommended to any student of Newton. A rather complete bibliography of Newton scholarship, divided into convenient categories, is printed as part of my *DSB* article (1974). Two other bibliographies of major recent Newtonian scholarship, chiefly in relation to my own research, are to be found in my *Introduction* (1971) and my *Newtonian revolution* (1980). A volume currently in press, edited by Zev Bechler and being published by Reidel, containing articles by Whiteside, Westfall, Dobbs, myself, and others, will certainly serve as a good review of current Newtonian scholarship in a variety of fields (with bibliographical guides). Two earlier surveys of the state of Newtonian scholarship are Cohen (1960) and Whiteside (1962). See also the important collection of Newtonian studies edited by Robert Palter (1970).

17. The penultimate sentence of the final scholium of Book Two of Newton's *Principles* reads: "Therefore the hypothesis of vortices can in no way be reconciled with astronomical phenomena and serves less to clarify the celestial motions than to obscure them."

18. In the commentary to the French translation of Newton's *Principles* (1759), vol 2, second part, p 9, it is said: "This second Book, which contains a very profound theory of fluids and the motions of bodies in fluids, seems to have been intended to destroy the system of vortices, although it is only in the scholium to the last Proposition that M.

Newton overtly attacks Descartes and shows that the celestial motions cannot be carried out by his vortices."

119. Brewster (1855), vol 1, 22, n 1, states: "Newton's copy of Descartes' Geometry I have seen among the family papers. It is marked in many places with his own hand, *Error, Error, non est Geom.*" Since this volume did not appear among either the books given by Lord Portsmouth to the University Library, Cambridge, nor in the auction sale, it came to be believed that Brewster had been wholly in error and that no copy with these annotations existed. See, further, note 127 *infra.*

120. This is the untitled essay which the Halls called "De gravitatione et aequipondio fluidorum" and which they published in their 1962 volume (pp 89-156), with translation and commentary.

121. See especially the long essay on Newton and Descartes in Koyré (1965), which, together with its appendixes, makes up half of the volume.

122. Cohen (1964).

123. See Cohen (1980), 186-7.

124. For the texts of Descartes compared and contrasted to the texts of Newton, see Cohen (1980), 183-4.

125. Koyré (1965), 66-70.

126. Cohen (1964).

127. The copy of Descartes' *Géométrie* in Latin in which Newton made his annotations was found a few years ago among some books that had at one time been destined to be discarded from the Trinity College Library.

128. Guerlac has developed these ideas in a number of publications, some of which are published in Guerlac (1977*a*); his ideas have been revised and summarized in his biography of Hauksbee in the *DSB.*

129. See note 128 *supra*; see also Koyré (1960). The final queries of the second (1717-18) English edition of the *Opticks* first appeared in the Latin *Opticae* (1706). The rise and fall of Newton's ideas concerning the aether and the experiments of Newton relating to this topic have been studied by R.S. Westfall and others, most recently in Cohen (1980) and in a long essay contributed to the volume (in press) being edited by Zev Bechler (see note 116 *supra*). Important studies of Newton's ideas of the aether, chiefly in relation to electricity, have been made by the Halls and by Joan L. Hawes. Zev Bechler has made a number of studies of Newton's optical ideas, based upon the manuscripts, and in particular has explored Newton's attempt to explain various optical phenomena by means of mathematical-physical models. Other important studies of Newton's optical experiments and ideas have been made by J.A. Lohne, who has in particular made an extensive study of the experimental conditions of Newton's prism experiments. Alan Shapiro has published several studies on aspects of Newton's work in optics and is currently

preparing an edition of Newton's *Lectiones opticae*. Valuable insights into the topic of Newton's views of the aether have been provided by Peter Heimann.

30. See Westfall (1971).
31. McGuire & Rattansi (1966).
32. McGuire (1967, 1968).
33. See the various writings of Manuel listed in the bibliography.
34. The mechanical philosophy associated with the name of Descartes gained wide adherence in the days of Newton. There can be no doubt that Newton was strongly influenced by the mechanical philosophy and sought indeed to explain all natural occurrences by means of matter and motion; when Newton disagreed with the Cartesian point of view, it was because he was a convinced atomist and thus believed in the existence of the vacuum or void space, which Descartes could not imagine to exist.
35. Westfall (1971), 377: "The significance of the redirection of his philosophy of nature undertaken by Newton about 1679 can scarcely be overstated." Newton's addition of the concept of force to the traditional concepts of the Cartesian mechanical philosophy had been suggested earlier by the Halls (1962). For a somewhat contrasting view of Newton's philosophy and the possible redirection of it, see my *Newtonian revolution* (1980) and the essay in the volume edited by Bechler (cited in note 116 *supra*).
36. See Westfall (1970).
37. See Lohne (1961, 1965, 1967, 1968); also Lohne & Sticker (1969). Shapiro's edition of the *Lectiones opticae* has not yet appeared. He has recently given a general summary of his ideas concerning optical problems of Newton in an article in *Isis* (1980).
38. This has been particularly brought out in Lohne (1965).
39. See Bechler's articles in the bibliography.
40. Westfall's ideas are most readily available in his recent biography (1980).
41. Manuel (1974).
42. Newton's early derivation is adumbrated in the last paragraph of the scholium to prop. 4, book 1, of his *Principles*. This paragraph was not part of the original MS, but was added while Halley was editing Newton's MS for publication. See the edition of Newton's *Principles* with variant readings (1972).
43. Herivel (1960, 1965).
44. In query 30 of the *Opticks*, Newton says: "The changing of Bodies into Light, and Light into Bodies, is very conformable to the Course of Nature, which seems delighted with Transmutations."
45. See the bibliography. An excellent bibliographical essay for this area is to be found in Dobbs (1975).

146. See, in particular, Boas & Hall (1958), M.B. Hall (1975).
147. Westfall (1972, 1975).
148. Dobbs (1975), Figala (1977, 1977a).
149. See, for example, Whiteside's review of Dobbs (1975) in *Isis* (1977), vol 68, pp 116–21.
150. On this subject, see Rattansi (1972); this whole area of the relation of Newton's interests in alchemy to the development of his thought in mechanics is treated in my article, forthcoming in the volume edited by Bechler (see note 116 *supra*).
151. Westfall (1975), p 196.
152. Dobbs (1975), pp 211, 221.
153. On this subject, see Hill (1965), p 7.
153a. Although studies of alchemy are important for opening up an examination of a major aspect of Newton's intellectual concerns, and although it is clear that alchemical questions are directly related to the nature of aether and Newton's conceptions of matter, a Scottish verdict of "non-proven" must be given to the assertions now being made that Newton's hermetic or alchemical concerns and thinking led him to universal gravity. Here, it seems to me, a gross error is made in not distinguishing between an understanding of terrestrial gravity (or weight) and the concept of universal gravity or the force produced by universal gravitation. In one case, that of weight, all that is required is some kind of process that draws bodies toward the earth. For instance, Newton himself advanced explanations of this phenomenon in terms of a shower of aetherial particles and later on in terms of an aether of varying degrees of density. I see no reason why the kind of "forces" that are related to or involved in alchemical processes could not be a source of an explanation of this kind of weight — in which, be it noted, there is no need of specifying whether a body is pushed toward the earth, pulled toward the earth, or gets acted on so as to be moved toward the earth by a mutual interaction between it and the earth.

In the case of universal gravity, however, the situation is entirely different. Here it is necessary not only to have a process that impels an object (such as a rock, an apple, or the moon) toward the earth, but one that at the same time impels the earth toward the object (whether a rock or an apple or a moon). There is nothing that I am familiar with in Newton's considerations of an alchemical kind that would have led to such a mutual interaction.

Furthermore, the steps that led Newton toward universal gravity were conditioned by considerations that began with the idea of a force directed toward a center where there was no body. This was related to the question proposed by Hooke to Newton in their correspondence in 1679–80, which set Newton going on the path that led him to universal gravity and finally to the *Principles*. This notion came to Newton not from considerations of alchemy, but rather directly from a question put to him by Robert Hooke. Newton's early solution was to begin by considering the orbital motion of a particle about an abstract center of force — a situation for which there is no analogue whatsoever in alchemy. It was only after Newton had developed such a system (not really a system, since there is only one body in it), that he recognized that in nature (as in the solar system) there is never a single body, but always a pair of bodies. For instance, the sun is at the center of the motion of the earth, the earth at the center of the motion of its moon; the sun is at the center of the motion of Jupiter, and Jupiter at the center of the motion of its moons. In any such system of two bodies, as Newton was quick to realize, the law of action and reaction (Newton's "third law") requires that the action be mutual, that if the sun is pulling on the earth, then the earth must be pulling on the sun with a force equal in magnitude but opposite in direction. And it is the same for the earth and its moon and even for the earth and an apple. Eventually, by a series of arguments of this kind, Newton was led to a principle of mutual interacting forces and to universal gravity — a process in which alchemical considerations are conspicuously absent. These topics are further developed in my *Newtonian revolution* (1980), my article on this topic in *Scientific American* (1981), and the article in the forthcoming volume edited by Bechler (cited in note 116 *supra*).

54. For details, see my *Introduction* (1971, ch 3, section 7).

55. Newton (1715), 206.

56. For instance, Newton said specifically that by "the inverse Method of Fluxions I found in the year 1677 [should be 1679/80] the demonstration of Kepler's Astronomical Proposition viz. that the Planets move in Ellipses, which is the eleventh Proposition of the first book of the Principles." See my *Introduction* (1971), 80, 289-98.

57. See Newton (1972), ix; see also my *Introduction* (1971). For further information concerning these volumes, see Harrison (1978).

57a See Newton (1972), 550-63. "Hypothesis 1" and "Hypothesis 2" of the first edition became "Rule 1" and "Rule 2" in the second edition. "Hypothesis 3" of the first edition was omitted in the second edition, where a wholly new "Rule 3" was introduced. A "Rule 4" appears for the first time in the third edition.

"Hypothesis 4" of the first edition became "Hypothesis 1" in the second and third editions and was removed to a later part of Book 3.

"Hypothesis 5" became "Phenomenon 1" in the second edition, where a wholly new "Phenomenon 2" was introduced. "Hypothesis 6 ... Hypothesis ‑9" became in the second edition "Phenomenon 3 ... Phenomenon 6." For the significance of these changes, see Cohen (1966).

157b One of the three "hypotheses" in the second and third editions of Newton's *Principles* was the original "Hypothesis 4," for which see n. 157a. Another, appearing also in Book 3 in the second and third editions (and there labeled "Hypothesis 2"), following prop. 38, was originally a "Lemma 4." Newton was unable to prove this lemma and so changed it to a hypothesis. According to Ball (1893), 110, "Laplace was the first writer to prove it." The third hypothesis in the second and third editions occurs at the beginning of section 9 of Book 2: "Hypothesis: The resistance which arises from the friction [*lit.*, lack of lubricity, ie, slipperiness] of the parts of a fluid is, other things being equal, proportional to the velocity with which the parts of the fluid are separated from one another." This hypothesis appeared identically in the first edition as well.

158. Newton, *Correspondence*, vol 2, p 309. This letter was part of the epistolary exchanges between Hooke and Newton during 1679 and 1680, in the course of which Hooke taught Newton that the proper way to analyze orbital motion was in terms of two components: a linear inertial component along the tangent to the curve and an accelerated motion directed toward the sun or center of force. See further my *Newtonian revolution* (1980), ch 5, sections 4–5.

159. See my *Newtonian revolution* (1980), 244–5; my *Introduction* (1971), 236–8; and Newton (1972). This alteration is summarized in Ball (1893), 100.

160. See my *Introduction* (1971), ch 9, section 4.

161. See Newton (1972), vol 2, app 1.

162. On this topic see the introduction to Newton (1975).

163. See Munby (1952).

163a See my *Introduction* (1971), pl. 13.

164. The copy with the author's name on the title page is in the library at the British Optical Society, London; see Sutcliffe (1932), where this title page is reproduced.

164a One of these belonged to Prof E.N. da C. Andrade and is described in Sotheby (1965), where the title page is reproduced on p 65; for the other, see Horblit (1964), section 54, with reproduction (in colour) of both forms of the title page.

164b This theme is developed in full in my *Newtonian revolution* (1980).

165. The best edition is that of F. Lefort and J.-B. Biot, i.e., Collins (1856); see Hall (1980) and vol 8 of Whiteside's edition of Newton's *Math. papers*.

166. U.L.C. MS Add. 3968.

166a See Hoskin (1961).

167. In addition to the one in the Royal Society and the three in the University Library, Cambridge, there is presumably one in the Macclesfield collection.

BIBLIOGRAPHY

Editor's note: Where the bibliography contains more than one publication by the same author in a given year, these are distinguished, for brevity in notes and in cross-references, by a lower case letter following the date. See, e.g., Guerlac (1963) & (1963a)

Aiton, E.J. (1962). "The celestial mechanics of Leibniz in the light of Newtonian criticism." *Annals of Science, 18*, 31–41;
– 1964. "The celestial mechanics of Leibniz: a new interpretation." *Annals of Science, 20*, 111–23.
– 1964a. "The inverse problem of central forces." *Annals of Science, 20*, 81–99.
– 1965 [1966]. "An imaginary error in the celestial mechanics of Leibniz." *Annals of Science, 21*, 169–73.
– 1969. "Kepler's second law of planetary motion." *Isis, 60*, 75–90.
– 1972. *The vortex theory of planetary motions*. London: Macdonald; New York: American Elsevier.
– 1975a. "The elliptical orbit and the area law." *Vistas in Astronomy, 18*, 573–83.
Andrade, E.N. Da C. 1935. "Newton's early notebook." *Nature, 135*, 360.
– 1950. "Wilkins lecture, Robert Hooke." *Proceedings of the Royal Society, 201A*, 439–73.
– 1953b. "A Newton collection." *Endeavour, 12*, 68–75.
– *See also* Sotheby. 1965.
Axtell, James, L. 1965. "Locke, Newton, and the elements of natural philosophy." *Paedagogica Europaea, 1*, 235–44.
– 1965a. "Locke's review of the *Principia*." *Notes and Records of the Royal Society of London, 20*, 152–61.
Babson Collection. 1950. *A descriptive catalogue of the Grace K. Babson collection of the works of Sir Isaac Newton, and the material relating to him in the Babson Institute Library, Babson Park, Mass.* Intro. Roger Babson Webber. New York: Herbert Reichner. Supplement compiled by Henry P. Macomber, Babson Institute, 1955.
Ball, W.W. Rouse. 1891. "On Newton's classification of cubic curves." *Proceedings of the London Mathematical Society, 22*, 104–43.
– 1892. "A Newtonian fragment relating to centripetal forces." *Proceedings of the London Mathematical Society, 23*, 226–31.
– 1893. *An essay on Newton's "Principia"*. London, New York: Macmillan. Photo-reprint, introd. I.B. Cohen. New York, London: Johnson, 1972.
– 1893a. *A short account of the history of mathematics*. 2nd ed.

London, New York: Macmillan. Contains an excellent chapter (16, pp 319–58), "The life and works of Newton."

— 1918. *Cambridge papers*. London: Macmillan.

Bechler, Zev. 1978. "Newton's search for a mechanistic model of colour dispersion: a suggested interpretation." *Archive for History of Exact Sciences, 11*, 1–37.

— 1974. "Newton's law of forces which are inversely as the mass: a suggested interpretation of his later efforts to normalise a mechanistic model of optical dispersion." *Centaurus, 18*, 184–222.

— 1974a. "Newton's 1672 optical controversies: a study in the grammar of scientic dissent." In *Elkana*. ed. 1974. pp 115–42.

— 1975. " 'A less agreeable matter': the disagreeable case of Newton and achromatic refraction." *British Journal for the History of Science, 8*, 101–26.

Biot, J. -B., and F. Lefort. *See* Collins et al., 1856.

Boas, Marie. 1958. "Newton's chemical papers." In *Newton*, 1958, 241-8.

— *See also* Hall, Marie Boas.

Boas, Marie, and A. Rupert Hall. 1958."Newton's chemical experiments." *Archives Internationales d'Histoire des Sciences, 11*, 113–52.

— *See also* Hall and Hall.

Brewster, Sir David. 1855. *Memoirs of the life, writings, and discoveries of Sir Isaac Newton*. 2 vols. Edinburgh: Thomas Constable. Photo-reprint, intro. Richard S. Westfall. New York, London: Johnston, 1965.

Brougham, Henry, Lord, and E.J. Routh. 1855. *Analytical view of Sir Isaac Newton's "Principia"*. London: Longman, Brown, Green, and Longmans, [&] C. Knight; Edinburgh: A. and C. Black; Glasgow: R. Griffin. Reprinted New York, London: Johnson, 1972.

Brunet, Pierre. 1929. *Maupertuis*. [1] Etude biographique. [2] L'oeuvre et sa place dans la pensée scientifique et philosophique du XVIIIe siècle. Paris: Librairie Scientifique Albert Blanchard.

— 1931. *L'introduction des théories de Newton en France au XVIIIe siècle*. Vol.I, avant 1738. Paris:Librairie Scientifique Albert Blanchard.

Buchdahl, Gerd. 1961. *The image of Newton and Locke in the age of reason*. London, New York: Sheed and Ward.

— 1973. "Explanation and gravity." In Teich and Young. 1973. pp 167-203.

Chandler, Philip P., II. 1975. Newton and Clairaut on the motion of the lunar apse. Diss. San Diego: University of California.

Cohen, I. Bernard. 1946. "Authenticity of scientific anecdotes." *Nature, 157*, 196-7.

— 1956. *Franklin and Newton: an inquiry into speculative Newtonian experimental science and Franklin's work in electricity as an example thereof.* Philadelphia: American Philosophical Society. Reprint Cambridge [Mass.] : Harvard University Press, 1966.

— 1960. "Newton in the light of recent scholarship." *Isis, 51*, 489-514.

— 1962. "The first English version of Newton's 'Hypotheses non fingo'." *Isis, 53*, 379-88.

— 1963. "Pemberton's translation of Newton's *Principia*, with notes on Motte's translation." *Isis, 54*, 319-51.

— 1964. "Isaac Newton, Hans Sloane, and the Académie Royale des Sciences." In Cohen and Taton, eds.. 1964, pp 61-116.

— 1964a. " 'Quantum in se est': Newton's concept of inertia in relation to Descartes and Lucretius." *Notes and Records of the Royal Society of London, 19*, 131-55.

— 1966. "Hypotheses in Newton's philosophy." *Physis, 8*, 163-84.

— 1967. "Dynamics: the key to the 'new science' of the seventeenth century." *Acta Historiae Rerum Naturalium necnon Technicarum.* Czechoslovak Studies in the History of Science. Prague, Special Issue 3, 79-114.

— 1967a. "Galileo, Newton, and the divine order of the solar system." In *Galileo, man of science.* Edited by E. McMullin. New York, London: Basic Books, 1967, pp 207-31.

— 1967b. "Newton's attribution of the first two laws of motion to Galileo." *Atti del Symposium Internazionale di Storia, Metodologia, Logica e Filosofia della Scienza, "Galileo nella Storia e nella Filosofia della Scienza,"* xxv-xliv. Collection des Travaux de l'Académie Internationale d'Histoire des Sciences, No. 16. Vinci (Florence): Gruppo Italiano di Storia della Scienza.

— 1969. Introduction to Newton. 1969. pp vii-xxii.

— 1969a. "Isaac Newton's *Principia*, the scriptures and the divine providence." In *Essays in honor of Ernest Nagel: philosophy, science and method.* Edited by Morgenbesser, Suppes, and White. New York, St. Martin's Press, pp 523-48.

— 1969b. "The French translation of Isaac Newton's *Philosophiae naturalis principia mathematica* (1756, 1759, 1966)." *Archives Internationales d'Histoire des Sciences, 72*, 37-67.

— 1969c. "Newton's *System of the world*: some textual and bibliographical notes." *Physis, 11*, 152-66.

— 1970. "Newton's second law and the concept of force in the *Principia*." In Palter, ed. 1970. pp 143-85. A considerably revised and corrected version of a preliminary text published in *Texas Quarterly, 10*, No. 3 (1967).

— 1971. *Introduction to Newton's "Principia".* Cambridge [Mass.] ;

Harvard University Press; Cambridge [England] : Cambridge University Press.

- 1972. "Newton and Keplerian inertia: an echo of Newton's controversy with Leibniz." In Debus, ed. 1972, 2, 199–211.
- 1974. "Newton, Isaac." *Dictionary of Scientific Biography, 10*, 42–103. Rev. and enl. ed. forthcoming, New York: Scribner's.
- 1974a. "Isaac Newton, the calculus of variations, and the design of ships: an example of pure mathematics in Newton's *Principia*, allegedly developed for the sake of practical applications." In R.S. Cohen et al., eds. 1974. pp 169–87.
- 1974b. "Newton's theory vs. Kepler's theory and Galileo's theory: an example of a difference between a philosophical and a historical analysis of science." In Elkana, ed.1974. pp 299–338.
- 1975. Bibliographical and historical introduction, in Newton. 1975. pp 1–87.
- 1979. "Notes on Newton in the art and architecture of the Enlightenment." *Vistas in Astronomy, 22* (pt. 4), 523–37.
- 1980. *The Newtonian revolution, with illustrations of the transformation of scientific ideas.* Cambridge [England] ; London, New York, New Rochelle: Cambridge University Press.
- 1981. "Newton's discovery of gravity." *Scientific American, 244*, No. 3 (March), 166–79.

Cohen, I. Bernard and Robert E. Schofield. *See* Newton. 1958.
Cohen, I. Bernard and René Taton, eds. 1964. *Mélanges Alexandre Koyré*. Vol. 1, *L'aventure de la science*; Vol. 2, *L'aventure de l'esprit*. Paris: Hermann, Histoire de la Pensée, Nos. 12 and 13.
- *See also* Koyré and Cohen. 1960, 1961, 1962.
Cohen, R.S., J.J. Stachel, and M.W. Wartofsky, eds. 1974. *For Dirk Struik. Scientific, historical and political essays in honor of Dirk J. Struik*. Boston Studies in the Philosophy of Science,Vol.15,Dordrecht, Boston: D. Reidel Publishing Company.
Collins, John, et al. 1856. *Commercium epistolicum J. Collins et aliorum de analysi promota, etc., ou, Correspondance de J. Collins et d'autres savants célèbres du XVIIe siècle, relative à l'analyse supérieure, réimprimée sur l'édition originale de 1712 avec l'indication des variantes de l'édition de 1722, complétée par une collection de pièces justificatives et de documents, et publiée par J.-B. Biot et F. Lefort*. Paris: Mallet-Bachelier.
Cotes, Roger. *See* Edleston, 1850.
Craig, Sir John. 1946. *Newton at the Mint*. Cambridge [England] : Cambridge University Press.
De Beer, G.R. *See* McKie and De Beer. 1952.

De Morgan, Augustus. 1848. "On the additions made to the second edition of the Commercium epistolicum," *Philosophical Magazine, 32,* 446–56.

— 1852. "On the authorship of the account of the Commercium epistolicum, published in the Philosophical Transactions." *Philosophical Magazine, 3,* 440–4.

— 1885. *Newton: his friend: and his niece.* London: Elliot Stock.

— 1914. *Essays on the life and work of Newton.* Edited, with notes and appendices, by Philip E.B. Jourdain. Chicago, London: Open Court Publishing Company.

De Villamil, R. 1931. *Newton: the man.* London: Gordon D. Knox.

Debus, Allen G., ed. 1972. *Science, medicine and society: essays to honor Walter Pagel.* 2 vols. New York: Science History Publications, Vol. 1 contains an appreciation of Pagel by Debus (pp 1–9); vol. 2 contains a bibliography of the writings of Pagel by Marianne Winder (pp 289–326).

Dobbs, Betty Jo Teeter. 1975. *The foundations of Newton's alchemy, or "The hunting of the greene lyon".* Cambridge [England] , London, New York, Melbourne: Cambridge University Press.

Domson, Charles Andrew. 1972. "Nicolas Fatio de Duillier and the prophets of London: an essay in the historical interaction of natural philosophy and millennial belief in the age of Newton." Diss. New Haven: Yale University.

Dreyer, J.L.E. 1924. "Address delivered by the President, Dr. J.L.Ē. Dreyer, on the desirability of publishing a new edition of Isaac Newton's collected works." *Monthly Notices of the Royal Astronomical Society, 84,* 298–304.

Edleston, J. 1850. *Correspondence of Sir Isaac Newton and Professor Cotes, including letters of other eminent men, now first published from the originals in the Library of Trinity College, Cambridge; together with an appendix, containing other unpublished letters and papers by Newton.* London: John W. Parker; Cambridge [England] : John Deighton.

Elkana, Yehuda, ed. 1974. *The interaction between science and philosophy.* Atlantic Highlands, N.J.: Humanities Press.

Figala, Karin. 1977. *Die "Kompositionshierarchie" der Materie — Newtons quantitative Theorie und Interpretation der qualitativen Alchemie.* Munich: unpublished Habilitationsschrift in the Technische Universität.

— 1977a "Newton as alchemist." *History of Science, 15,* 102–37. Essay based on Dobbs. 1975.

Fraser, Duncan C. 1919. *Newton's interpolation formulas.* London: C.

dE. Layton. Identical in content to Fraser's articles in *The Journal of the Institute of Actuaries, 51* (Oct. 1918), 77–106, (Apr. 1919), 211–32. Supplementary material from Newton's *MSS* was published in *58* (Mar. 1927), 53–95, and was then included in a reprint of the earlier work under the same title in 1927 (London: C. dE. Layton).

Gabbey, Alan [W. Allan]. 1971. "Force and inertia in seventeenth-century dynamics." *Studies in History and Philosophy of Science, 2*, 1–67.

— 1976. "Essay review of Newton. 1972." *Historia Mathematica, 3*, 237–43.

Geoghegan, D. 1957. "Some indications of Newton's attitude towards alchemy." *Ambix, 6*, 102–6.

Gray, George J. 1907. *A bibliography of the works of Sir Isaac Newton, together with a list of books illustrating his works.* 2d. ed. rev. and enl. Cambridge [England] : Bowes and Bowes.

Greenstreet, W.J. ed. 1927. *Isaac Newton, 1642–1727. A memorial volume edited for the Mathematical Association.* London: G. Bell and Sons.

Gregory, David. 1937. *David Gregory, Isaac Newton and their circle, extracts from David Gregory's memoranda 1677–1708.* Edited by W.G. Hiscock. Oxford: printed for the editor.

Gregory, James Craufurd. 1832. "Notice concerning an autograph manuscript by Sir Isaac Newton, containing some notes upon the third book of the *Principia*, and found among the papers of Dr David Gregory, formerly Savilian Professor of Astronomy in the University of Oxford." *Transactions of the Royal Society of Edinburgh, 12*, 64–76.

Guerlac, Henry. 1963. "Francis Hauksbee: Expérimentateur au profit de Newton." *Archives Internationales d'Histoire des Sciences, 16*, 113–28.

— 1963a. *Newton et Epicure.* Paris: Palais de la Découverte [Histoire des Sciences: D–91].

— 1964. "Sir Isaac and the ingenious Mr. Hauksbee." In Cohen and Taton, eds. 1964. 1. 228–53.

— 1967. "Newton's optical aether. His draft of a proposed addition to his *Opticks*." *Notes and Records of the Royal Society of London, 22*, 45–57.

— 1972. "Hales, Stephen." *Dictionary of Scientific Biography, 6*, 35–48.

— 1972a. "Hauksbee, Francis." *Dictionary of Scientific Biography, 6*, 169–75.

— 1973. "Newton and the method of analysis." In *Dictionary of the history of ideas, 3.* Edited by Philip P. Wiener. New York: Scribner's,

378-91.

— 1977. "The Newtonianism of Dortous de Mairan." In *Essays on the age of enlightenment in honor of Ira O. Wade.* Edited by Jean Macary, Geneva: Librairie Droz, 131-41.

— 1977a. *Essays and papers in the history of science.* Baltimore, London: Johns Hopkins University Press. Contains most of Guerlac's early papers on Newton and the aether, on the *Opticks,* and on Hauksbee and Newton, but not (alas!) Guerlac (1972).

— 1981. *Newton on the continent.* Ithaca: Cornell University Press.

Hall, A. Rupert. 1948. "Sir Isaac Newton's note-book, 1661-1665." *Cambridge Historical Journal, 9,* 239-50.

— 1957. "Newton on the calculation of central forces." *Annals of Science, 13,* 62-71.

— 1980. *Philosophers at war: the quarrel between Newton and Leibniz.* Cambridge [England] , London, New York, New Rochelle: Cambridge University Press.

Hall, A. Rupert and Marie Boas Hall. 1959. "Newton's electric spirit: four oddities." *Isis, 50,* 473-76.

— 1959a. "Newton's 'mechanical principles'." *Journal of the History of Ideas, 20,* 167-78.

— 1960. "Newton's theory of matter." *Isis, 51,* 131-44.

— 1961. "Clarke and Newton." *Isis, 52,* 583-5.

— eds. 1962. *Unpublished scientific papers of Isaac Newton. A selection from the Portsmouth Collection in the University Library, Cambridge.* Cambridge [England] : Cambridge University Press.

Hall, Marie Boas. 1975. "Newton's voyage in the strange seas of alchemy." In Righini Bonelli and Shea, eds. 1975. 239-46.

— *See also* Boas, Marie.

Harrison, John. 1978. *The library of Isaac Newton.* Cambridge [England] , London, New York, Melbourne: Cambridge University Press.

Hawes, Joan L. 1968. "Newton and the 'electrical attraction unexcited'." *Annals of Science, 24,* 121-30.

Heimann, Peter M. 1973. " 'Nature is a perpetual worker': Newton's aether and 18th-century natural philosophy." *Ambix, 20,* 1-25.

Herivel, J.W. 1960. "Newton's discovery of the law of centrifugal force." *Isis, 51,* 546-53.

— 1960a. "Suggested identification of the missing original of a celebrated communication of Newton's to the Royal Society." *Archives Internationales d'Histoire des Sciences, 13,* 71-8.

— 1961. "Interpretation of an early Newton manuscript." *Isis, 52,* 410-16.

— 1961a. "The originals of the two propositions discovered by Newton in December 1679?" *Archives Internationales d'Histoire des Sciences, 14*, 23-33.

— 1962. "Early Newtonian dynamical *MSS.*" *Archives Internationales d'Histoire des Sciences, 15*, 149-50.

— 1965. *The background to Newton's "Principia." A Study of Newton's dynamical researches in the years 1664-84*. Oxford: Clarendon Press.

— 1965*a*. "Newton's first solution to the problem of Kepler motion." *British Journal for the History of Science, 2*, 350-4.

Hill, Christopher. 1965. *Intellectual origins of the English revolution*. Oxford: Clarendon Press.

Horblit, Harrison D. 1964. *One hundred books famous in science*. Based on an exhibition held at the Grolier Club. New York: Grolier Club.

Horsley, Samuel. *See* Newton. 1779-.

Hoskin, Michael. 1961. "The mind of Newton." *The Listener, 66* (19 October), 597-9.

Huxley, G.L. 1959. "Two Newtonian studies, I — Newton's boyhood interests; II — Newton and Greek geometry." *Harvard Library Bulletin, 13*, 348-61.

Huygens, Christiaan. 1888-. *Oeuvres complètes de Christiaan Huygens*. Publiées par la Société Hollandaise des Sciences. The Hague: Martinus Nijhoff. Vol. 22: Supplément à la correspondance, varia, biographie de Chr. Huygens..., published in 1950.

Koyré, Alexandre. 1939. *Etudes galiléennes*. Paris: Hermann & Cie. Reprinted 1966.

— 1950. "The significance of the Newtonian synthesis." *Archives Internationales d'Histoire des Sciences, 3* [29], 291-311.

— 1952. "An unpublished letter of Robert Hooke to Isaac Newton." *Isis, 43*, 312-37.

— 1955. "Pour une édition critique des oeuvres de Newton." *Revue d'Histoire des Sciences, 8*, 19-37.

— 1956. "L'hypothèse et l'expérience chez Newton." *Bulletin de la Société francais de Philosophie, 50*, 59-79.

— 1960. "Newton, Galileo, and Plato." *Actes du IXe Congrès International d'Histoire des Sciences*, Barcelona-Madrid, 1959, 165-97. Reprinted in *Annales: Economies, Sociétés, Civilisations*, Vol. 6, 1041-59, and in Koyré. 1965. pp 201-20.

— 1960*a*. "Les queries de l'Optique." *Archives Internationales d'Histoire des Sciences, 13*, 15-29.

— 1960*b*. "Les Regulae philosophandi." *Archives Internationales d'Histoire des Sciences, 13*, 3-14.

— 1965. *Newtonian studies*. Cambridge [Mass.] : Harvard University

Press; London: Chapman & Hall. More than half the volume consists of a previously unpublished study, "Newton and Descartes," pp 53–200.

— 1966. *Etudes d'histoire de la pensée scientifique.* Paris: Presses Universitaries de France.

Koyré, Alexandre and I. Bernard Cohen. 1960. "Newton's 'electric & elastic spirit'." *Isis, 51,* 337.

— 1961. "The case of the missing *tanquam*: Leibniz, Newton and Clarke." *Isis, 52,* 555–66.

— 1962. "Newton & the Leibniz-Clarke correspondence, with notes on Newton, Conti, and Des Maizeaux." *Archives Internationales d'Histoire des Sciences, 15,* 63–126.

Lagrange, Joseph Louis. 1788. *Méchanique analytique.* Paris: chez la veuve Desaint, Librairie.

— 1797. *Théorie des fonctions analytiques, contenant les principes du calcul différentiel, dégagés de toute considération d'infiniment petits ou d'évanouissans, de limites ou de fluxions, et réduits à l'analyse algébrique des quantités finies.* Paris: Impr. de la République [prairial an V].

Larmor, Joseph. 1924. "On editing Newton." *Nature, 113,* 744.

Lefort, F., and J.-B. Biot. *See* Collins et al. 1856.

Lohne, Johannes A. 1960. "Hooke versus Newton. An analysis of the documents in the case of free fall and planetary motion." *Centaurus, 7,* 6–52.

— 1961. "Newton's 'proof' of the sine law." *Archive for History of Exact Sciences, 1,* 389–405.

— 1965. "Isaac Newton: the rise of a scientist 1661-1671." *Notes and Records of the Royal Society of London, 20,* 125–39.

— 1967. "The increasing corruption of Newton's diagrams." *History of Science, 6,* 69–89.

— 1968. "Experimentum crucis." *Notes and Records of the Royal Society of London, 23,* 169–99.

Lohne, Johannes A., and Bernhard Sticker. 1969. *Newtons Theorie der Prismenfarben mit Ubersetzung und Erläuterung der Abhandlung von 1672.* Munich: Werner Fritsch.

Mach, Ernst. 1926. *The principles of physical optics, an historical and philosophical treatment.* Trans. John S. Anderson and A.F.A. Young. London: Methuen. Reprinted New York: Dover, 1953.

— 1960. *The science of mechanics: a critical and historical account of its development.* Trans. Thomas J. McCormack, new introduction by Karl Menger, 6th ed., with revisions through 9th German ed. La Salle, [Ill.]: Open Court Publishing Co.

Malone, Dumas. 1948. *Jefferson the Virginian*. Boston: Little, Brown.

Manuel, Frank E. 1959. *The eighteenth century confronts the gods.* Cambridge [Mass.] : Harvard University Press.

— 1963. *Isaac Newton, historian.* Cambridge [Mass.] : Harvard University Press, Belknap Press.

— 1968. *A portrait of Isaac Newton.* Cambridge [Mass.] : Harvard University Press, Belknap Press.

— 1974. *The religion of Isaac Newton.* Oxford: Clarendon Press.

McGuire, J.E. 1966. "Body and void and Newton's *De mundi systemate*: some new sources." *Archive for History of Exact Sciences, 3,* 206–48.

— 1967. "Transmutation and immutability: Newton's doctrine of physical qualities." *Ambix, 14,* 69–95.

— 1968. "The origin of Newton's doctrine of essential qualities." *Centaurus, 12,* 233–60.

McGuire, J.E. and P.M. Rattansi. 1966. "Newton and the 'pipes of Pan'." *Notes and Records of the Royal Society of London, 21,* 108–43.

— *See also* Westman and McGuire, 1977.

McKie, Douglas, and G.R. De Beer. 1952. "Newton's apple." *Notes and Records of the Royal Society of London, 9,* 46–54, 333–5.

McLachlan, Herbert, ed. *See* Newton. 1950.

McMullin, Ernan. 1978. *Newton on matter and activity.* Notre Dame [Indiana] , London: University of Notre Dame Press.

Miller, Perry. 1958. "Bentley and Newton." In Newton. 1958. pp 271–8.

Mills, A.A. 1981."Newton's prisms and his experiments on the spectrum." *Notes and Records of the Royal Society of London, 36,* 13–36.

Mills, A.A. and P.J. Turvey. 1979. "Newton's Telescope." *Notes and Records of the Royal Society of London, 33,* 133–55.

More, L.T. 1934. *Isaac Newton: a biography.* New York, London: Scribner's. Reprinted. New York: Dover.

Motte, Andrew. *See* Newton. 1729. 1934.

Munby, A.N.L. 1951, 1952. "The two title-pages of the *Principia*." *Times Literary Supplement, 50* (21 December), 2603; *51* (28 March), 228.

— 1952*a.* "The distribution of the first edition of Newton's *Principia*." *Notes and Records of the Royal Society of London, 10,* 28–39.

— 1952*b.* "The Keynes Collection of the works of Sir Isaac Newton at King's College, Cambridge." *Notes and Records of the Royal Society of London, 10,* 40–50.

Napier, John. 1889. *The construction of the wonderful canon of logarithms.* Translated from Latin into English, with notes and a catalogue of the various editions of Napier's works, by William Rae MacDonald. Edinburgh, London: William Blackwood and Sons.

Newton, Isaac. 1672. "A letter of Mr. Isaac Newton ... containing his new theory about light and colors." *Philosophical Transactions, 6*, 3075–87.

— 1702. *A new and most accurate theory of the moon's motion; whereby all her irregularities may be solved, and her place truly calculated to two minutes.* Written by the incomparable mathematician Mr. Isaac Newton, and published in Latin by Mr. David Gregory in his excellent astronomy. London: printed and sold by A. Baldwin. Reprinted in Newton. 1975.

— 1715. "[Recensio Libri=] An account of the book entituled *Commercium epistolicum Collinii & aliorum, de analysi promota*, published by order of the Royal-Society, in relation to the dispute between Mr. Leibnits and Dr. Keill, about the right of invention of the new method of fluxions, by some call'd the differential method." *Philosophical Transactions, 29*, 173–224. The title of the book given in the *Philosophical Transactions* is not the exact title of the *Commercium epistolicum* [first edition] itself. A French translation appeared in the *Journal Littéraire*, Nov./Dec. 1715, vol. 6, pp 13 ff, 345 ff.

— 1728. *A treatise of the system of the world.* Translated into English. London: printed for F. Fayram.

— 1728a. *De mundi systemate liber.* London: impensis J. Tonson, J. Osborn, & T. Longman.

— 1728b. *Optical lectures read in the publick schools of the University of Cambridge, anno Domini, 1669.* By the late Sir Isaac Newton, then Lucasian Professor of the Mathematicks. Never before printed. Translated into English out of the original Latin. London: printed for Francis Fayram.

— 1729. *The mathematical principles of natural philosophy.* Translated into English by Andrew Motte. *To which are added, The laws of the moon's motion, according to gravity.* By John Machin. In two volumes. London: printed for Benjamin Motte. Facsimile reprint, intro. I. Bernard Cohen. London: Dawsons of Pall Mall, 1968.

— 1733. *Observations upon the prophecies of Daniel and the Apocalypse of St. John.* London: printed by J. Darby and T. Browne.

— 1759. *Principes mathématiques de la philosophie naturelle.* Translated "par feue Madame la Marquise du Chastellet." 2 vols. Paris: chez Desaint & Saillant [& chez] Lambert.

— 1779–. *Opera quae exstant omnia.* Commentariis illustrabat Samuel Horsley. 5 vols. London: John Nichols. Volume 5 was published in 1785. 5 vol. reprinted in 1964. Stuttgart-Bad Cannstatt. Friedrich Verlag (Günther-Holzboog).

- 1931. *Opticks or a treatise of the reflections, refractions, inflections & colours of light.* Reprinted from the fourth edition [London, 1730]. Foreword by Prof. Albert Einstein, Nobel Laureate. Introduction by Prof. E.T. Whittaker, F.R.S. London: G.Bell & Sons.
- 1934. *Sir Isaac Newton's Mathematical principles of natural philosophy and his System of the world.* Translated into English by Andrew Motte in 1729. The translations revised, and supplied with an historical and explanatory appendix, by Florian Cajori. Berkeley: University of California Press.
- 1950. *Theological manuscripts.* Edited by H. McLachlan. Liverpool: University Press.
- 1952. *Opticks or a treatise of the reflections, refractions, inflections & colours of light.* Based on the fourth edition: London, 1730. With foreword by Albert Einstein; Introduction by Sir Edmund Whittaker; Preface by I. Bernard Cohen; Analytical table of contents prepared by Duane H.D. Roller. New York: Dover Publications.
- 1958. *Isaac Newton's papers & letters on natural philosophy and related documents.* Edited, with a general introduction, by I. Bernard Cohen assisted by Robert E. Schofield. Cambridge [Mass.] : Harvard University Press. 2d ed., rev. and enl. Harvard University Press, 1978.
- 1959-1977. *The correspondence of Isaac Newton.* Vol 1, 1661-1675 (1959), vol 2, 1676-1687 (1960), vol 3, 1688-1694 (1961), Edited by H.W. Turnbull; vol 4, 1694-1709 (1967), Edited by J.F. Scott; vol 5, 1709-1713 (1975), vol 6, 1713-1718 (1976), vol 7, 1718-1727 (1977), Edited by A. Rupert Hall and Laura Tilling. Published for the Royal Society. Cambridge [England] : Cambridge University Press.
- 1964-1967. *The mathematical works of Isaac Newton.* Assembled with an introduction by Dr. Derek T. Whiteside. 2 vols. New York, London: Johnson Reprints [The Sources of Science].
- 1967-. *The mathematical papers of Isaac Newton.* Vol 1, 1664-1666 (1967); vol 2, 1667-1670 (1968); vol 3, 1670-1673 (1969); vol 4, 1674-1684 (1971); vol 5, 1683-1684 (1972); vol 6, 1684-1691 (1974); vol 7, 1691-1695 (1976); Edited by D.T. Whiteside, with the assistance in publication of M.A. Hoskin and A. Prag. Cambridge: Cambridge University Press. To be complete in 8 vols.
- 1969. *A treatise of the system of the world.* Translated into English. With an introduction by I.B. Cohen. London: Dawsons of Pall Mall. Photo-reprint of the 2d ed. (1731), plus the front matter of the 1st ed. (1728).
- 1972. *Isaac Newton's Philosophiae naturalis principia mathematica.* the third edition (1726) with variant readings assembled by Alexandre Koyré, I. Bernard Cohen, & Anne Whitman. 2 vols. Cambridge

[England] : Cambridge University Press; Cambridge [Mass.] : Harvard University Press.
— 1973. *The unpublished first version of Isaac Newton's Cambridge lectures on optics 1670-1672.* A facsimile of the autograph, now Cambridge University Library *MS.* Add. 4002, with an introduction by D.T. Whiteside. Cambridge [England] : The University Library.
— 1975. *Isaac Newton's "Theory of the moon's motion" (1702).* With a bibliographical and historical introduction by I. Bernard Cohen. London: Dawson.
Palter, Robert. 1970. "Newton and the inductive method." In Palter, ed. 1970. pp 244-57.
— ed. 1970. *The annus mirabilis of Sir Isaac Newton 1666-1966.* Cambridge [Mass.] , London: M.I.T. Press.
Patterson, Louise Diehl. 1949, 1950. "Hooke's gravitation theory and its influence on Newton. I: Hooke's gravitation theory. II: The insufficiency of the traditional estimate." *Isis, 40,* 327-41; *41,* 32-45.
Pighetti, Clelia. 1960. "Cinquant' anni di studi newtoniani(1908-1959)." *Rivista Critica di Storia della Filosofia,* fascicoli 2-3, 181-203, 295-318.
Portsmouth Collection. 1888. *A catalogue of the Portsmouth Collection of books and papers written by or belonging to Sir Isaac Newton, the scientific portion of which has been presented by the Earl of Portsmouth to the University of Cambridge.* Prepared by H.R. Luard, G.G. Stokes, J.C. Adams, and G.D. Liveing. Cambridge [England] : Cambridge University Press.
Priestley, F.E.L. 1970. "The Clarke-Leibniz controversy." In *The methodological heritage of Newton.* Edited by Robert E. Butts and John W. Davis. Oxford: Basil Blackwell, pp 34-56.
Rattansi, P.M. 1972. "Newton's alchemical studies." In Debus, ed. 1972. Vol. 2, pp 167-82.
— 1973. "Some evaluations of reason in sixteenth- and seventeenth-century natural philosophy." In Teich and Young, eds. 1973. pp 148-66.
Rigaud, Stephen Peter. 1838. *Historical essay on the first publication of Sir Isaac Newton's "Principia".* Oxford: Oxford University Press. Reprinted, New York, London: Johnson 1972.
— ed. 1841. *Correspondence of scientific men of the seventeenth century ... in the collection of ... the Earl of Macclesfield.* 2 vols. Oxford: Oxford University Press.
Righini Bonelli, M.L. and William R. Shea, eds. 1975. *Reason, experiment, and mysticism in the scientific revolution.* New York: Science History Publications.

Royal Society. 1947. *Newton tercentenary celebrations.* Cambridge [England] : Cambridge University Press. Contains E.N. da C. Andrade, "Newton"; Lord Keynes, "Newton, the man"; J. Hadamard, "Newton and the infinitesimal calculus"; S.I. Vavilov, "Newton and the atomic theory"; N. Bohr, "Newton's principles and modern atomic mechanics"; H.W. Turnbull, "Newton: the algebraist and geometer"; W. Adams, "Newton's contributions to observational astronomy"; J.C. Hunsaker, "Newton and fluid mechanics."

Ruffner, James Alan. 1966. "The background and early development of Newton's theory of comets." Diss. Bloomington: Indiana University.

— 1971. "The curved and the straight: cometary theory from Kepler to Hevelius." *Journal for the History of Astronomy, 2,* 178-95.

Sabra, A.I. 1967. *Theories of light from Descartes to Newton.* London: Oldbourne.

Sampson, R.A. 1924. "On editing Newton." *Monthly Notices of the Royal Astronomical Society, 84,* 378-83.

Schofield, Robert E. 1958. "Halley and the *Principia.*" In Newton. 1958. pp 397-404.

Scott, J.F. *See* Newton. 1959-1977.

Shapiro, Alan E. 1980. "The evolving structure of Newton's theory of white light and color." *Isis, 71,* 211-35.

Smith, David Eugene. 1927. "Two unpublished documents of Sir Isaac Newton." In *Isaac Newton, 1642-1727.* Edited by W.J. Greenstreet. London: G. Bell and Sons, pp 16-34.

Sotheby & Co. 1936. *Catalogue of the Newton papers, sold by order of the Viscount Lymington to whom they have descended from Catherine Conduitt, Viscountess Lymington, great-niece of Sir Isaac Newton.* London: Sotheby & Co.

— 1965. *Catalogue of the fine collection of scientific books, the property of Professor E.N. da C. Andrade, F.R.S.* London: Sotheby & Co.

Stukeley, William. 1936. *Memoirs of Sir Isaac Newton's life, 1752: being some account of his family and chiefly of the junior part of his life.* Edited by A. Hastings White. London: Taylor and Francis.

Sutcliffe, John H., comp. and ed. 1932. *British Optical Association Library and Museum catalogue.* London: Council of the British Optical Association.

Taylor, F. Sherwood. 1956. "An alchemical work of Sir Isaac Newton." *Ambix, 5,* 59-84.

Teich, Mikulas and Robert Young, eds. 1973. *Changing perspectives in the history of science: essays in honour of Joseph Needham.* London: Heinemann.

Turnbull, Herbert Westren, ed. 1939. *James Gregory: tercentenary memorial volume. Containing his correspondence with John Collins and his hitherto unpublished mathematical manuscripts, together with addresses and essays communicated to the Royal Society of Edinburgh, July 4, 1938.* Published for the Royal Society of Edinburgh. London: G. Bell and Sons.

— 1951. "The discovery of the infinitesimal calculus." *Nature, 167,* 1048-50.

— 1953. "Isaac Newton's letters: some discoveries." *Manchester Guardian,* 3 October, p 4. Reprinted, *Manchester Guardian Weekly,* 8 October, p 11.

— *See also* Newton. 1959-1977.

Turnor, Edmund. 1806. *Collections for the history of the town and soke of Grantham, containing authentic memoirs of Sir Isaac Newton, now first published from the original MSS, in the possession of the Earl of Portsmouth.* London: William Miller.

Waff, Craig. 1975. *Universal gravitation and the motion of the moon's apogee: the establishment and reception of Newton's inverse-square law, 1687-1749.* Diss. Baltimore: Johns Hopkins University.

— 1967. "Isaac Newton, the motion of the lunar apogee, and the establishment of the inverse square law." *Vistas in Astronomy, 20,* 99-103.

Wallis, Peter and Ruth Wallis. 1977. *Newton and Newtoniana, a bibliography.* Folkestone [Kent, England] : Dawson.

Westfall, Richard S. 1962. "The foundations of Newton's philosophy of nature." *British Journal for the History of Science, 1,* 171-82.

— 1963. "Newton's reply to Hooke and the theory of colors." *Isis, 54,* 82-96.

— 1963a. "Short-writing and the state of Newton's conscience, 1662." *Notes and Records of the Royal Society of London, 18,* 10-16.

— 1967. "Uneasily fitful reflections on fits of easy transmission." *Texas Quarterly, 10,* No. 3 (Autumn), 86-102.

— 1967a. "Hooke and the law of universal gravitation." *The British Journal for the History of Science, 3,* 245-61.

— 1970. "Uneasily fitful reflections on fits of easy transmission." In Palter, ed. 1970. 88-104.

— 1971. *Force in Newton's physics: the science of dynamics in the seventeenth century.* London: Macdonald; New York: American Elsevier.

— 1972. "Newton and the hermetic tradition." In Debus, ed. 1972. 2, 183-98.

— 1973. "Newton and the fudge factor." *Science, 179,* 751-8.

— 1975. "The role of alchemy in Newton's career." In Righini

Bonelli and Shea, eds. 1975. pp 189-232.

— 1980. *Never at rest, a biography of Isaac Newton.* Cambridge [England], London, New York, New Rochelle: Cambridge University Press.

Westman, Robert S., and J.E. McGuire. 1977. *Hermeticism and the scientific revolution.* Los Angeles: University of California, William Andrews Clark Memorial Library.

Whiteside, Derek T. 1961. "Newton's discovery of the general binomial theorem." *Mathematical Gazette, 45,* 175-80.

— 1961a. "Patterns of mathematical thought in the later seventeenth century." *Archive for History of Exact Sciences, 1,* 179-388.

— 1962. "The expanding world of Newtonian research." *History of Science, 1,* 16-29.

— 1964. "Isaac Newton: birth of a mathematician." *Notes and Records of the Royal Society of London, 19,* 53-62.

— 1964a. "Newton's early thoughts on planetary motion: a fresh look." *British Journal for the History of Science, 2,* 117-37.

— 1966. "Newtonian dynamics." *History of Science, 5,* 104-17. Review article on Herivel. 1965.

— 1966a. "Newton's marvellous year: 1666 and all that." *Notes and Records of the rRoyal Society of London, 21,* 32-41.

— 1970. "Before the *Principia*: the maturing of Newton's thoughts on dynamical astronomy, 1664-84." *Journal for the History of Astronomy, 1,* 5-19.

— 1970a. "The mathematical principles underlying Newton's *Principia.*" *Journal for the History of Astronomy, 1,* 116-38.

— 1976. "Newton's lunar theory: from high hope to disenchantment." *Vistas in Astronomy, 19,* 317-28.

— 1977. "From his claw the greene lyon." *Isis, 68,* 116-21. Essay-review of Dobbs. 1975.

— *See also* Newton. 1964-1967, 1967-.

Wightman, W.P.D. 1953. "Gregory's 'Notae in Isaaci Newtoni Principia Philosophiae'." *Nature, 172,* 690.

Wilson, Curtis. 1970. "From Kepler's laws, so-called, to universal gravitation: empirical factors." *Archive for History of Exact Sciences, 6,* 89-170.

— 1974. "Newton and some philosophers on Kepler's 'laws'." *Journal of the History of Ideas, 35,* 231-58.

Witting, Alexander. 1911-12. "Zur Frage der Erfindung des Algorithmus der Newtonschen Fluxionsrechnung." *Bibliotheca Mathematica,* series 3, Vol. 12, 56-60.

Zeitlinger, H. 1927. "A Newton bibliography." In Greenstreet. ed. 1927. pp 148-70.

Members of the Conference

Margaret Anderson, *University of Toronto*
M. and Mme. Armand Beaulieu, *Gouvieux, France*
G.E. Bentley, Jr., *University College, University of Toronto*
Kenneth Blackwell, *The Bertrand Russell Archives, McMaster University*
William Blissett, *University College, University of Toronto*
Laura Braswell, *McMaster University*
Betsey B.P. Buchwald, *University of Toronto*
Jed Z. Buchwald, *University of Toronto*
I. Bernard Cohen, *Harvard University*
Jane Couchman, *Glendon College, York University*
J.A. Dainard, *University College, University of Toronto*
A.H. De Quehen, *University of Toronto*
Stillman Drake, *University of Toronto*
Alvin I. Dust, *University of Waterloo*
Hilda Gifford, *Carleton University*

Victor E. Graham, *University of Toronto*
Nicholas Griffin, *McMaster University*
Bert S. Hall, *University of Toronto*
Bert Hansen, *University of Toronto*
W.H. Herendeen, *University of Toronto*
William L. Hine, *Atkinson College, York University*
Evelyn J. Hinz, *University of Manitoba*
F. David Hoeniger, *Victoria College, University of Toronto*
J.N.P. Hume, *Massey College, University of Toronto*
H.J. Jackson, *Scarborough College, University of Toronto*
J.R. de Jackson, *Victoria College, University of Toronto*
John Lancaster, *Amherst College*
Richard G. Landon, *Thomas Fisher Rare Book Library, University of Toronto*
Trevor H. Levere, *University of Toronto*
Roger C. Lewis, *Acadia University*
Pauline M.H. Mazumdar, *University of Toronto*
Ruth Mortimer, *Smith College*
Desmond Neill, *Massey College, University of Toronto*
Jonathan Pearl, *University of Toronto*
Richard A. Rempel, *McMaster University*
A.G. Rigg, *University of Toronto*
ViAnn Shewchek, *Toronto*
Noel Swerdlow, *University of Chicago*
Philip M. Teigen, *McGill University*
Ron B. Thomson, *University of Toronto*
Linda E. Voigts, *University of Missouri — Kansas City*
Germaine Warkentin, *Victoria College, University of Toronto*
Philip J. Weimerskirch, *Burndy Library, Norwalk*
Judith Williams, *University of Toronto Press*
Milton Wilson, *Trinity College, University of Toronto*
George J. Zytaruk, *Nipissing University College*

Selected Index